REWARD
Resource Pack

REVIVAL

Intermediate (B1/B2)

Written by Sue Kay

Published by ELT Teacher 2 Writer

Worksheet	Interaction	Skills	Aim	Time	Grammar & functions	Vocabulary
1 Spotlight on you	Whole class	Writing Speaking	Getting to know one another To write a question for each student in the class To ask and answer questions	20–30	Questions without a question word Questions with a question word	Personal information
2 Find out	Whole class	Speaking	Getting to know one another To find out information about members of the class by asking and answering questions	15–20	Asking for and giving information Questions with a question word: *what, when, who, how* Questions without a question word and with an auxiliary verb	Personal information
3 What are you doing next week?	Whole class	Speaking	To make plans for the following week and arrange times and places to meet other members of the class	20–30	Present continuous to talk about definite arrangements in the future	Leisure activities
4 Relationship stories	Pairwork	Reading Speaking	To practise talking about relationships	30–40	Describing a sequence of events	Stages of a relationship
5 Half-minute topics	Groupwork	Speaking	To play a board game by speaking about given topics	30–40	Talking about likes and dislikes Verb patterns *to* or *-ing* *Would like to/love to* + infinitive to talk about ambitions, hopes and preferences Adverbs and adverbial phrases of frequency	Routine and leisure activities
6 Are you on the same wavelength?	Pairwork	Speaking	To see how well students know each other by predicting a partner's answers to questions about their musical taste	20	Adjectives ending in *-ed* and *-ing* Question tags Short answers	Types of music and other music-related topics
7 Find someone who …	Whole class	Speaking	To ask and answer questions and to complete a chart	15–20	Questions without a question word and with an auxiliary verb Adjectives ending in *-ed* and *-ing* Verb patters: *to* or *-ing*	General
8 Sentences in a hat	Whole class	Writing Speaking	To complete unfinished sentences To pick sentences out of a hat and find out who wrote them by asking questions	20	Questions without a question word and with an auxiliary verb Adjectives ending in *-ed* and *-ing*	General
9 Best of friends	Groupwork	Writing	To create a story by inventing answers to questions and writing them down	30–40	Past simple to talk about a past action or event that is finished Past continuous to talk about something that was in progress at a specific time in the past	Personal qualities
10 I'm different now	Pairwork	Writing Speaking	To talk about yourself as a child, and to compare the way things were with the way they are now	20–30	*Used to* + infinitive to talk about past habits, routines and states which are now finished	Personal information

Worksheet	Interaction	Skills	Aim	Time	Grammar & functions	Vocabulary
11 When in Rome	Whole class	Speaking Reading Writing	To put a story in the correct order by saying and listening to sentences To write the story down in a group dictation	45	Telling a story: *when, as soon as, as, while* *When* and *as soon as* + past simple for actions which happen one after the other *When, as* and *while* + past continuous for longer actions	A journey
12 Really?!	Pairwork	Writing Speaking	To write imaginary information about people by completing unfinished sentences	20	Non-defining relative clauses with *who* for giving additional information about people	General
13 Problems, problems, problems	Whole class (Mill drill)	Speaking	To speak to as many partners as possible, making complaints, apologising and making requests	15–20	Complaining: *I'm sorry …, I'm afraid …* Apologising Responding to apologies Making requests	General
14 Dominoes	Groupwork	Speaking	To play a game of dominoes matching adjectives and their strong equivalents	20–30	Base and strong adjectives, for example: *angry – furious, cold – freezing*	Adjectives
15 Around the world	Pairwork Groupwork	Speaking Writing	To talk about things you've done and things you haven't done yet by playing a card game	35–45	Present perfect simple: *already, yet, still*	Leisure activities, cities and countries
16 How long …?	Whole class	Speaking	To find out how long people have been doing things by asking and answering questions	15–20	Present perfect simple or continuous for asking and saying how long	General
17 Comparisons	Groupwork	Speaking	To make comparisons using cards	15–20	Making comparisons: comparative adjective + *than*; *more/less* + comparative adjective + *than*; *more* + countable /uncountable noun + *than*; *fewer* + plural countable noun + *than*; *less* + uncountable noun + *than*; *as much* + uncountable noun + *as*; *as many* + plural countable noun + *as*; *as* + adjective + *as*	General
18 Describing objects	Groupwork	Speaking	To play a board game by using adjectives in the correct order when describing objects	30	Order of adjectives and phrases for describing objects	Adjectives for describing opinion, size, age, shape, colour, origin and material
19 What's in your wardrobe?	Pairwork	Speaking Writing	To ask and answer questions about your clothes	20–30	Talking about your clothes	Clothes
20 Predict your future	Whole class	Speaking Writing	To ask and answer questions about the future and to create a group poster	20	Making predictions: certainty, probability, possibility Certain: *I'm sure I will, I definitely won't* Probable: *I probably will/won't* Possible: *I might*	Everyday activities

Worksheet	Interaction	Skills	Aim	Time	Grammar & functions	Vocabulary
21 Can you do it?	Groupwork	Speaking	To find out what people can do by asking and answering questions	20–30	*Can* to talk about general ability in the present	General
22 It says in the contract …	Groupwork	Reading Speaking Writing	To write an imaginary contract for teachers	20–30	Modal verbs: *should, must* for giving advice; *have to, must, mustn't* for obligation *don't have to* for lack of obligation; *be supposed to* to talk about what people are expected to do because of a rule or tradition	School rules
23 Film review	Groupwork	Speaking Writing	To write reviews of imaginary films by looking at pictures which could be film posters	45	Adjectives and adverbs: *amazing – amazingly, beautiful – beautifully*, etc. Giving opinions: *I thought it was really good/funny. I found it interesting/boring*, etc. Emphasising: *absolutely, extremely, really*, etc.	Types of film, parts of a film, adjectives to describe a film
24 My life as an animal	Pairwork	Writing Speaking	To pretend you're an animal and to give personal information as if you were that animal. To guess what animal other people are pretending to be.	15–20	Position of adverbs and adverb phrases Adverbs of manner: *well, badly* Adverb phrases of time: *in the last/next few days; after supper*	Animals and the way they live their lives
25 Love is …	Pairwork	Speaking	To categorise quotes about love and to discuss attitudes to being in love	20–30	Reported speech *Said (that)* + clause	Love and relationships
26 Who asked me that?	Groupwork	Speaking Writing	To ask and answer the questions and then to remember who asked which questions	30	Reported speech: questions *Asked* + clause Direct questions and reported questions with question words (*who, what, how, which, where*) and without question words	General
27 Reported speech dominoes	Pairwork	Writing Speaking	To play a game of dominoes by matching direct and reported statements	35–45	Reported speech Reporting verbs: *encourage, agree, decide, promise, apologise, invite, warn, offer, refuse, remind, advise, ask, tell, suggest*	General
28 Holiday crossword	Pairwork	Speaking Writing	To write clues for a crossword and complete it	30	Defining relative clauses beginning with *who, that, which, where* or *whose*	Words associated with holidays
29 Jobs at home	Whole class (Mill drill)	Speaking	To speak to as many partners as possible about jobs that need doing around the home	15–20	*Need + -ing* and passive infinitive Causative construction with *have* and *get: have something done, get something done*	Household jobs
30 If I could change the world …	Whole class	Writing Speaking	To write about and discuss what you would do if you were in different positions of authority	30	*Make* + noun/pronoun + infinitive to express obligation; *Let* + noun + infinitive to express permission; *Not let* to express prohibition	General

Worksheet	Interaction	Skills	Aim	Time	Grammar & functions	Vocabulary
31 Spot the wrong word	Pairwork	Speaking	To identify and correct lexical mistakes in sentences	20–30	Commonly confused words	Words which are often confused: *come–go, lend–borrow, bring–take, sensible–sensitive, check–control, leave–forget, watch–see, hear–listen to, expect–wait for, loose–lose*
32 Describe it	Groupwork	Speaking	To play a board game by describing and guessing words	30–40	Describing things when you don't know the word: *It's a place where …; someone who …; something that …; something you use to …; something you do …*	Useful objects, general revision
33 How many uses can you think of?	Groupwork	Writing Speaking	To invent unusual uses for ordinary objects	20–30	Infinitive of purpose: *to +* infinitive to say how you do something; *By + -ing* to say how you do something; *Use it as a …*; Give advice: *If +* present simple to describe a problem and what to do about it	Useful objects
34 If you come here	Groupwork	Reading Writing Speaking	To read information and to write notes about it To choose a place you want to visit	40–50	First conditional to talk about a likely situation and to talk about its results	Description of places, scenery and lifestyle
35 A mysterious connection	Pairwork	Speaking Writing	To dictate part of a story and to write down what your partner dictates to you	20–30	Past perfect simple to talk about one action in the past which happened before another action in the past Past perfect continuous when you want to focus on an action which was in progress up to or near a time in the past, rather than a completed event	Narrative
36 Holiday choices	Pairwork	Speaking	To categorise vocabulary and to discuss what you look for in a holiday	20–30	*My holiday priorities are …; I'm not a fan of …; When I'm on holiday I like/don't like to …; If x happened, I'd …*	Holidays
37 Dear Sue	Pairwork	Speaking Writing	To practise talking about relationships	30–40	Expressions for giving advice: *If I were you I'd …; I think you should/ought to …; In my opinion, you should/ought to …*	Personal relationships and life in general
38 What went wrong?	Whole class (Mill drill)	Speaking	To speak to as many partners as possible, commenting on things that went wrong on holiday	20–30	Past modals: *should have* and *shouldn't have*	Holiday activities Travel
39 If only I'd taken more chances	Whole class	Writing Speaking	To imagine you're 87 years old and to talk about past regrets	30	Expressing regrets about the past with *I wish / If only + past perfect*	General
40 Imagine	Whole class	Writing Speaking	To write sentences about imaginary situations in the past and their results To pick sentences out of a hat and find out who wrote them by asking questions	20	Third conditional to talk about an imaginary or unlikely situation in the past and to describe its result	General

Mill drills

There are several mill drills in the Resource Pack.

What is a mill drill?

A mill drill is an interactive way of drilling newly presented language, using cards with picture or word prompts on one or both sides. It fulfils the function of repetition and substitution drills. As the name suggests, the students stand up and 'mill' (circulate) around the class, interacting with several partners. It's an ideal way of providing controlled practice of a new structure or function after initial presentation, because it gives students the opportunity to repeat the same language with several different partners.

The benefits of a mill drill for the student

The presentation stage of a lesson can be teacher-centred and static. A mill drill makes a welcome change of focus for both students and teacher. It makes controlled practice more communicative and enjoyable for students and basic repetition becomes more stimulating and active. A mill drill can also be reassuring for less confident students, not only because the students are solely dependent on mechanical repetition and substitution but also because they are not required to speak alone.

The benefits of a mill drill for the teacher

Mill drills differ from conventional drills in that they are student-centred, providing an invaluable opportunity for the teacher to monitor individual students' weaknesses, particularly pronunciation and intonation.

How to do a mill drill with your class

There are instructions for each mill drill in the Teacher's Notes accompanying each mill drill worksheet. The basic procedure is as follows:

Preparation

1. Print a copy of the worksheet and cut out the cards as indicated. With a large class, divide the class into groups and print one copy of the worksheet for each group.

2. Give each student a card. It is not necessary to use all the cards on the worksheet, so if there are fewer students in the class or group than the number of cards on the worksheet, leave out the surplus number. Follow the instructions in the Teacher's Notes carefully.

Demonstration

1. Tell students that they are going to spend 10–15 minutes practising the new language and that you are going to demonstrate.

2. Give one card to each student in the class, and keep one for yourself. Select a sample dialogue and write it on the board, preferably eliciting the language from students. Indicate the part of the dialogue to be supplied by the picture or word prompt on the card. For example:

[Card showing a person reading.]
A: Do you like reading?
B: Yes, I do.
A: So do I.

3. Explain that this language will change according to the prompt on the card, and elicit suggestions for this. For example: *Do you like reading / playing tennis / listening to podcasts?*

4. Show students how to hold their cards. This is particularly important when using double-sided cards which must be held up at eye level so that when students are talking to a partner they are both able to see each other's cards and the relevant prompts.

5. Choose a confident student to demonstrate the activity with you. Then ask two or three pairs of students to demonstrate the dialogue.

Students do the mill drill

Ask all the students to stand up and go round the class or group, repeating the dialogue with as many different partners as possible, using their cards as prompts.

Some mill drills have two stages involving either turning the cards round, or exchanging cards with another student so that students get the opportunity to make new responses. In these mill drills, tell students that they should stop talking when you clap your hands and continue once they have made the necessary change.

A mill drill is a controlled practice activity and it is important that students use the language accurately. So, while students are doing the task, you should circulate, listening and correcting any mistakes in grammar and pronunciation.

1 Spotlight on you

Questions for	Questions asked by
(Name) _____	(Name) _____

What's your favourite _____? _____

Have you ever _____? _____

Where do you usually _____? _____

Are you _____? _____

Do you have _____? _____

Do you _____? _____

How old _____? _____

What are you going to _____? _____

When did you _____? _____

Do you think you'll _____? _____

Would you like to _____? _____

_____? _____

_____? _____

1 Spotlight on you

ACTIVITY
Whole class: writing, speaking

AIMS
Getting to know one another
To write a question for each student in the class
To ask and answer questions

GRAMMAR AND FUNCTIONS
Questions without a question word and with an auxiliary verb
Questions with a question word: what, *when*, *where*, *how* and an auxiliary verb

VOCABULARY
Personal information

TIME
20 to 30 minutes

PREPARATION
Make one copy of the worksheet for each student in the class.

PROCEDURE
1. If there are more than 12 students in the class, divide them into groups. It's easier if the students in each group are seated in a circle or a semi-circle for this activity, but this is not essential.

2. Give a copy of the worksheet to each student.

3. Ask students to write their own name at the top of the worksheet in the space provided under the heading 'Questions for'.

4. Now ask students to give their worksheet to the person in their group who is sitting on their left.

5. Tell students that they are going to think of a question they would like to ask the person whose name is at the top of the worksheet they have received. They should write their question on the worksheet by completing one of the unfinished questions. They can choose any unfinished question they like.

6. When they have written a question, they should write their own name next to it in the space provided in the 'Questions asked by' column. They should then give the worksheet to the person on their left.

7. Repeat the activity until students receive the worksheet with their own name at the top again.

8. Now ask students to go round the class, find each of the students who wrote a question for them and answer it.

9. Make sure students know a polite way of refusing to answer questions, for example, *I'd rather not answer that*, and tell them that they have the right to remain silent!

2 Find out

What's the most popular colour?

FIND OUT.

What's the most popular leisure activity?

FIND OUT.

Who went to bed latest last night?

FIND OUT.

Who's got the longest surname?

FIND OUT.

Who's bought second-hand clothes?

FIND OUT.

Who had the busiest weekend?

FIND OUT.

Who's got the biggest family?

FIND OUT.

Who travels furthest to school/work/college?

FIND OUT.

Who's got the most unusual pet?

FIND OUT.

Who's been to the cinema most recently?

FIND OUT.

Who's going to have their birthday next?

FIND OUT.

What sort of music is most popular?

FIND OUT.

2 Find out

ACTIVITY
Whole class: speaking

AIMS
Getting to know one another
To find out information about members of the class by asking and answering questions

GRAMMAR AND FUNCTIONS
Asking for and giving information
Questions with a question word: *what, when, who, how*
Questions without a question word and with an auxiliary verb

VOCABULARY
Personal information

TIME
15 to 20 minutes

PREPARATION
Make one copy of the worksheet for each group of up to 12 students. Cut the cards out as indicated.

PROCEDURE
1. If there are more than 12 students in the class, divide them into groups. Give one card to each student in the class.

2. Tell students that they are responsible for finding the answer to the question on their own card by speaking to everybody in the class or group. Make sure each student understands the words on their card and knows how to ask the relevant questions correctly.

3. Now ask students to go round the class or group asking and answering questions. Tell them they can make notes on the back of their card if necessary.

4. When they have finished, they should sit down and take it in turns to report back to the class or group on what they found out during the activity.

FOLLOW-UP
Ask students to stay in their groups and write a summary of the information they have gathered to be displayed either on a poster in the classroom or on the school platform.

3 What are you doing next week?

	MORNING	AFTERNOON	EVENING
MONDAY	_____ with _____ at _____	_Bowling_ with _everyone in the class_ at _2.15_	_____ with _____ at _____
TUESDAY	_____ with _____ at _____	_____ with _____ at _____	_____ with _____ at _____
WEDNESDAY	_Yoga_ with _everyone in the class_ at _10.30_	_____ with _____ at _____	_Pizza evening_ with _everyone in the class_ at _7.30_
THURSDAY	_____ with _____ at _____	_____ with _____ at _____	_____ with _____ at _____
FRIDAY	_____ with _____ at _____	_____ with _____ at _____	_Quiz night_ with _everyone in the school_ at _8.30_
SATURDAY	_____ with _____ at _____	_____ with _____ at _____	_____ with _____ at _____
SUNDAY	_____ with _____ at _____	_Picnic_ with _everyone in the class_ at _1.30_	_____ with _____ at _____

3 What are you doing next week?

ACTIVITY
Whole class: speaking

AIM
To make plans for the following week and arrange times and places to meet other members of the class

GRAMMAR AND FUNCTIONS
Present continuous to talk about definite arrangements in the future

VOCABULARY
Leisure activities

TIME
20 to 30 minutes

PREPARATION
Make one copy of the worksheet for each student in the class.

PROCEDURE
1. Give a copy of the worksheet to each student in the class.

2. Tell students that this is a page out of their diary and that they are going to make some arrangements for the following week.

3. Ask each student to think of six leisure activities they would like to do during the week, and to write them down wherever they like in their diary. Point out the arrangements already written in the diary as examples, but explain that at this point they should only write in the activity and leave the spaces marked *with* and *at* blank.

4. When they have done that, ask students to go round the class and find someone who is free to do each of the activities with them. They should find a different person for each activity. Before they begin the activity, elicit the following example exchanges:

Student A: *What are you doing on Thursday evening?*
Student B: *Nothing. I'm free.*
Student A: *Would you like to come swimming with me?*
Student B: *Yes, I'd love to.*
Student A: *OK, let's meet at 6.30.*
Or
Student A: *What are you doing on Saturday afternoon?*
Student B: *I'm going to the cinema.*
Student A: *What about Saturday evening?* etc.

When Students A and B have agreed to do an activity together, they should write each other's names and the time they have arranged to meet in the relevant places in their diaries.

5. Students repeat the activity until they have found someone to do each of their leisure activities with.

6. Stop the activity when one student has finalised arrangements for each of their six leisure activities.

4 Relationship stories

You meet one another in person.	You decide to be exclusive.	You have children.
You fall in love.	You meet one another online.	Your families meet.
You get to know one another.	You go out with one another.	You're widowed.
You get married.	You get engaged.	You get divorced.
Your relationship ends.	You start living together.	You have a long-distance relationship.

Story A

Javi first met Carlos in high school. They immediately fell in love and went out with one another in their final year of school before going on to study at different colleges. They tried to keep a long distance relationship going, but in the end they lost touch and their relationship came to an end. They went into different careers that meant their paths didn't cross again. Javi never forgot Carlos though, and when he retired at the age of 63, he searched for his teenage sweetheart's name online, found him on social media and emailed him. They chatted for a while and Javi found out that Carlos had been widowed some years previously. After a while, Javi drove 500 kilometres to Carlos's home where they realised that it was never too late to find happiness.

Story B

During the Covid pandemic, Youssef signed up to a dating site and met Madeleine. Madeleine lived with her family in Lyon, France and Youssef lived with his brother in Marrakech, Morocco. They started video-calling one another every day, comparing experiences of living through the pandemic. Both were working remotely from home and Madeleine was also caring for her elderly mother. They got to know one another online and couldn't travel to meet one another because of the pandemic travel restrictions. They got engaged before meeting one another in person and as soon as the pandemic was over, Youssef travelled to France to meet Madeleine for the first time. Now they're married, and neither of them regrets their unusual engagement.

Story C

When Kelsey fell in love and got engaged to Michael, she had to learn a new language so she could communicate with his parents who were deaf. She hadn't met his family yet because Michael communicates with them using American Sign Language. Kelsey wanted to perform her wedding vows in sign language. She had 11 months to learn, and one of Michael's aunts helped her. The aunt was the only person who knew what Kelsey was planning for her wedding day. Kelsey was worried that she'd make a mistake and offend someone, but she practised a lot, and on the day, everything went well. Michael cried when he saw Kelsey signing, and thought it was one of the best moments of the day. The video went viral on social media. Now Kelsey has got to know Michael's family and is fluent in sign language.

4 Relationship stories

ACTIVITY
Pairwork: reading, speaking

AIM
To practise talking about relationships

GRAMMAR AND FUNCTIONS
Describing a sequence of events

VOCABULARY
Stages of a relationship

TIME
30 to 40 minutes

PREPARATION
- Make one copy of the complete worksheet and cut stories A, B and C off as indicated.
- Make one copy of the stages of a relationship at the top of the worksheet for each student in the class and cut them up as indicated.
- Make one copy of stories A, B and C for each group of three students in the class and cut them up as indicated.

PROCEDURE
1. Give one set of cut up stages of a relationship cards to each student. Do not give them stories A, B and C yet.

2. Ask students to read through the cards and check they know the meanings of all the phrases. Explain any new words or phrases.

3. Ask students to think of a relationship they, or somebody they know, has had. Tell them to arrange the relationship stages cards in the order in which they happened. Students don't need to use all of the stages, only the relevant ones. They can also add other stages if necessary.

4. When they have done that, ask students to work in groups of three and compare their relationship stories.

5. Ask for feedback: Were their stories similar or different? Was there anything they found particularly interesting? Were there any stages of a relationship missing from the list on the worksheet?

6. Ask students to stay in groups of three. One student is A, one is B and one is C. Give a copy of Story A to Student As, Story B to Student Bs and Story C to Student Cs. Ask students to read their story without showing it to the other students in their group.

7. Now ask each student to reorder the 'stages of a relationship' cards according to the story they've read.

8. Ask students to put away their stories and take it in turns to describe the relationship they have read about to the other students in their group. They should refer to the order in which they have arranged their 'stages of a relationship' cards to help them.

9. Ask students to say which story they found most interesting. Do they know anybody who's had a long-distance relationship or one that has overcome difficulties?

FOLLOW-UP
1. Ask students to put the following actions in order according to their own morning routine, leaving out any that are irrelevant:

get out of bed	put make-up on
put clothes on	check social media
put shoes on	read the news headlines
have breakfast	make the bed
have a shower	kiss members of your family
clean teeth	feed your pet
wash the dishes	take your dog for a walk
brush hair	say prayers

2. Ask students to compare their morning routines with a partner.

5 Half-minute topics

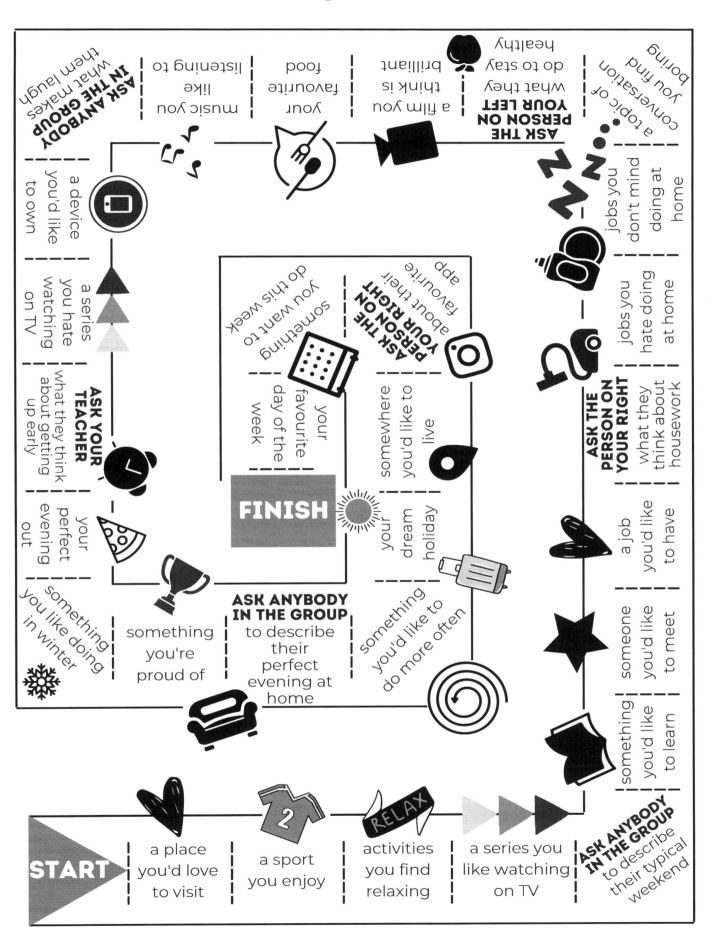

5 Half-minute topics

ACTIVITY
Groupwork: speaking

AIM
To play a board game by speaking about given topics

GRAMMAR AND FUNCTIONS
Talking about likes and dislikes
Verb patterns *to* or *-ing*
Would like to/love to + infinitive to talk about ambitions, hopes and preferences
Adverbs and adverbial phrases of frequency

VOCABULARY
Routine and leisure activities

TIME
30 to 40 minutes

PREPARATION
Make one copy of the worksheet for every four to six students in the class. Provide dice and counters for each group. Each group will also need a watch with second hands, or a stopwatch on their phone.

PROCEDURE
1. Ask students to work in groups of four to six.

2. Give one game board, some counters and a dice to each group.

3. Before students start playing the game, explain how to play using the instructions below. If you wish, you can make a copy of the instructions for each group, or display them to the class.

4. Start the game. While students are playing, go round to each group, check they are playing correctly and answer any language questions they may have.

HOW TO PLAY THE GAME
1. Put the game board in the middle of the table and set your stopwatch to zero.

2. All players put their counters on the square marked START and throw the dice. The first player to throw a six starts the game.

3. Player 1 throws the dice and moves their counter along the board according to the number on the dice.

4. Player 1 then reads the topic on the square the counter has landed on and talks about it for 30 seconds. Players should be timed from the point at which they start talking, allowing them a little thinking time before they start talking.

5. If a player lands on a square with the instruction to ask somebody else, they should read the topic aloud to the relevant person who then talks about it for 30 seconds.

6. If a player has nothing to say on the topic they have landed on, they are allowed to pass and miss a turn, but they can only do this once in the game.

7. The game continues in a clockwise direction until one player reaches the square marked FINISH.

6 Are you on the same wavelength?

_____ (partner's name)

Predict your partner's answers.

✓ = I was right
✗ = I was wrong

Q How do you discover new music?

A Through friends.　　Online.　　From reviews.　　☐

Q How often to you listen to classical music?

A Often.　　Sometimes.　　Never.　　☐

Q Do you sing in the bath or shower?

A Yes, I do.　　No, I don't.　　☐

Q Do you remember the lyrics of songs?

A Yes, I do.　　No, I don't.　　☐

Q Have you ever seen a band in a stadium?

A Yes, I have.　　No, I haven't.　　☐

Q What music have you got on your latest playlist?

A Chilled music.　　Rock music.　　A bit of everything.　　☐

Q What do you think of rap?

A I love it.　　It's ok.　　It's dreadful.　　☐

Q What do you think life would be like without music?

A Boring.　　Depressing.　　Peaceful.　　☐

Q Do your parents like the same music as you?

A Yes, they do.　　No, they don't.　　☐

Q How often do you listen to music while you're working?

A Always.　　Sometimes.　　Not often.　　☐

Q Is there anyone in your family who's a good musician?

A Yes, there is.　　No, there isn't.　　☐

Q What is your favourite music?

A _____　　☐

How many predictions did you get right? Score one point for each tick.
Read to see how well you know your partner. If you scored ...
1 to 5: You are not really on the same wavelength.
6 to 9: You know your partner's taste in music quite well – or you're good at guessing!
10 to 13: You're completely on the same wavelength as your partner.

6 Are you on the same wavelength?

ACTIVITY
Pairwork: speaking

AIM
To see how well students know each other by predicting a partner's answers to questions about their musical taste

GRAMMAR AND FUNCTIONS
Adjectives ending in -*ed* and -*ing*
Question tags
Short answers

VOCABULARY
Types of music and other music-related topics

TIME
20 minutes

PREPARATION
Make one copy of the worksheet for each student in the class.

PROCEDURE
1. Ask students to work in pairs.

2. Give one copy of the worksheet to each student in the class and ask students to write their partner's name in the space provided at the top of the worksheet.

3. Explain to students that they are going to find out how well they know one another by predicting their partner's answers to questions about music.

4. Ask students to circle or underline the answers they think their partner would give to each question on the worksheet without asking their partner yet.

5. Before students begin the pairwork stage, elicit sample exchanges such as:
Student A: *You discover new music through friends, don't you?*
Student B: *Yes I do.*
Student A: *You never listen to classical music, do you?*
Student B: *Actually, I sometimes listen to classical music.*

6. Now students should take it in turns to check whether they have guessed their partner's answers correctly.

7. Students should put a tick or a cross in the column provided next to each question depending on whether they have guessed correctly or not.

8. When students have finished checking their answers with their partner, they should add up their total number of right guesses and then read the score at the bottom of the worksheet.

9. Find out which student or students in the class made the most correct predictions.

7 Find someone who ...

Find someone who ...	Name
... plays a musical instrument.	_____
... likes baking.	_____
... has been to a wedding recently.	_____
... thinks watching football on TV is boring.	_____
... thinks social media is dangerous.	_____
... listens to music for more than an hour a day.	_____
... finds opera moving.	_____
... is terrified of spiders.	_____
... thinks cold showers are refreshing.	_____
... gets excited when they watch a basketball match.	_____
... feels relaxed when they go for a walk in the country or a park.	_____
... would like to learn to salsa dance.	_____

7 Find someone who ...

ACTIVITY
Whole class: speaking

AIM
To ask and answer questions and to complete a chart

GRAMMAR AND FUNCTIONS
Questions without a question word and with an auxiliary verb

Adjectives ending in *-ed* and *-ing*

Verb patterns: *to* or *-ing*

VOCABULARY
General

TIME
15 to 20 minutes

PREPARATION
Make one copy of the worksheet for each student in the class.

PROCEDURE
1. Give one copy of the worksheet to each student in the class.

2. Explain to students that they are going to transform the statements on their worksheet into questions and then go round the class asking one another the questions.

3. Ask students to work in pairs and give them a few moments to transform the statements on their worksheet into the questions they will ask, and ask them to write them on their worksheets. Check that questions have been formed correctly.

4. Ask students to go round the class individually, asking and answering questions. When they find someone who answers *yes* to a question, they put the person's name next to the statement in the space provided. It is important to tell the students that they can only put the same name twice. This is to encourage them to speak to as many different partners as possible.

5. When one student has found a name for each of the statements on the worksheet, stop the activity.

6. As a follow-up, ask students to say which statements were difficult to put a name to, and which were easy.

ANSWERS
Do you play a musical instrument?
Do you like baking?
Have you been to a wedding recently?
Do you think watching football on TV is boring?
Do you think social media is dangerous?
Do you listen to music for more than an hour a day?
Do you find opera moving?
Are you terrified of spiders?
Do you think cold showers are refreshing?
Do you get excited when you watch a basketball match?
Do you feel relaxed when you go for a walk in the country or a park?
Would you like to learn to salsa dance?

8 Sentences in a hat

Another language I'd like to learn is

_____

I think English grammar is

_____

I find

_____

confusing.

I think people who

_____

are amazing.

A country I'm interested in is

_____

When I'm embarrassed, I

_____

I'm frightened of

_____

I'm tired of

_____

I find

_____

incredibly boring.

I find

_____

inspiring.

I find

_____

extremely relaxing.

When I'm worried, I

_____

8 Sentences in a hat

ACTIVITY
Whole class: writing, speaking

AIM
To complete unfinished sentences
To pick sentences out of a hat and find out who wrote them by asking questions

GRAMMAR AND FUNCTIONS
Questions without a question word and with an auxiliary verb
Adjectives ending in -ed and -ing

VOCABULARY
General

TIME
20 minutes

PREPARATION
Make one copy of the worksheet for each group of three to four students in the class and cut it up as indicated. You will need a hat or a box for this activity (or two containers if there are 20 or more students in the class).

PROCEDURE
1. Choose one of the unfinished sentences from the worksheet and write it on the board. Elicit possible ways of completing the sentence. For example:
Another language I'd like to learn is Arabic.
I'm frightened of spiders.

2. Ask students to work in groups of three or four for the first part of the activity. Give one set of unfinished sentences to each group and ask students to spread out the pieces of paper face-down and to take three each.

3. Ask them to complete their three sentences in any way they like. (Refer to the examples in procedure step 1). They should not write their names or let the students next to them see what they are writing.

4. Students now all work together as a class. Put the hat (or box) in the middle of the room. If there are 20 or more students in the class, divide them into two groups and put a hat in the middle of each group. Ask students to fold up their completed sentences and put them in the hat.

5. Mix up the sentences in the hat and then tell students that they are all going to stand up, take a sentence each and find out who wrote it. Demonstrate by taking a piece of paper from the hat and reading the sentence out. For example:
Another language I'd like to learn is Arabic.

Elicit the question they will need to ask in order to find out who wrote the sentence:
Would you like to learn Arabic?

Ask the question until you find the person who wrote the sentence. Make it clear that even though students may answer *yes* to the question, they are looking for the person who wrote it, and may need to ask, *Did you write this sentence?*

6. Now ask students to stand up and take a piece of paper each from the hat. If they choose their own sentence, they should return it and pick again. Students are now ready to go round the class or group asking questions. All the students in the class do this simultaneously. While they are doing this, go round and offer help with formulating the questions correctly.

7. When a student finds the person who wrote the sentence, they should write the person's name on the piece of paper, keep it, and take another one from the hat. Students repeat the activity until there are no sentences left in the hat.

8. Ask students to sit down and count the number of completed sentences they have collected. The student with the most sentences is the winner.

9. Ask students to report back to the class on what they found out during the activity. For example:
Monica thinks English grammar is difficult.
Hassan finds wet weather incredibly boring.

9 Best of friends

When they first met, they never imagined they would become the best of friends because they were so different from one another.

Who was the woman?

_____

_____

fold -

Who was the man?

_____

_____

fold -

Where did they meet?

_____

_____

fold -

Where was she living, what was she doing, and how was she feeling when they first met?

_____

_____

fold -

Where was he living, what was he doing, and how was he feeling when they first met?

_____

_____

fold -

What did they talk about?

_____

_____

fold -

What did she like about him?

_____

_____

fold -

What did he like about her?

_____

_____

fold -

How long have they been friends?

_____

_____

9 Best of friends

ACTIVITY
Groupwork: writing

AIM
To create a story by inventing answers to questions and writing them down

GRAMMAR AND FUNCTIONS
Past simple to talk about a past action or event that is finished
Past continuous to talk about something that was in progress at a specific time in the past

VOCABULARY
Personal qualities

TIME
30 to 40 minutes

PREPARATION
Make one copy of the worksheet for each student or each pair of students in the class.

PROCEDURE
1. If there are more than 20 students in the class, divide them into groups. Students may work individually or in pairs. It is easier if the class or groups are seated in a circle or semi-circle, but this is not essential.

2. Tell students that they are going to write the story of a friendship between two people by inventing answers to some questions.

3. Give a copy of the worksheet to each student or pair of students in the class and ask them to write an answer to the first question in the space provided by inventing details.

4. When their first answer is complete, tell students to fold their piece of paper to the back so that the sentence they have written is hidden and the next question is visible. They should then give it to the student or pair of students on their left.

5. Ask students to write imaginary details in answer to the question which is now at the top of the page on the piece of paper they have received.

6. When they have done that, ask them to fold it as before and give it to the student or pair of students on their left.

7. Repeat the activity until all the questions have been answered. Encourage students to be as imaginative or as amusing as they like when they are writing their answers.

8. When the final question has been answered, ask students to open out the completed story they have received and read it. If there are any words or phrases that students do not understand or think are incorrect, tell them to find the student who wrote them and ask them to explain or correct the word or phrase.

9. Vote for the most amusing or interesting story in the group or class.

10 I'm different now

	Me as a child aged _____ (any age between 5 and 10)	Me now
What games / play?		
What TV series / watch?		
What hobbies / have?		
What pets / have?		
What music / like?		
What clothes / wear?		
What look / like?		
What / be like?		
What tech / use?		
What food / hate?		
What / be frightened of?		
What ambitions / have?		

10 I'm different now

ACTIVITY
Pairwork: writing, speaking

AIM
To talk about yourself as a child, and to compare the way things were with the way things are now

GRAMMAR AND FUNCTIONS
Used to + infinitive to talk about past habits, routines and states which are now finished

VOCABULARY
Personal information

TIME
20 to 30 minutes

PREPARATION
Make one copy of the worksheet for each student in the class.

PROCEDURE
1. Give one copy of the worksheet to each student in the class.

2. Ask each student to choose an age between 5 and 10 and to write it in the space provided on their worksheet.

3. Now ask students to write answers to the questions on their worksheet from the point of view of themselves as a child of the age they have chosen. They should write their answers under the heading, 'Me as a child aged ___'. At this stage you may need to remind students of the difference between *like* and *look like* and *be like*.

4. When they have answered all the questions in the first column, ask students to write answers to the same questions, but from the point of view of themselves now. They should write these answers under the heading, 'Me now'.

5. For the next part of the activity, ask students to work in pairs. They should take it in turns to ask and answer questions about the way things used to be when they were a child and the way things are now by referring to the rest of the information on their worksheets. Before this, elicit example conversations. Check that question formation is correct. For example:

Student A: *What games did you use to play?*
Student B: *I used to play with dolls at home and I used to play running games at school.*
Student B: *What hobbies did you use to have?*
Student A: *I used to go horse-riding.*
Student B: *What hobbies do you have now?*
Student A: *I go to the gym.*

In a class where the students come from a variety of different cultures, they may have to explain some of their answers to their partner; for example, games or TV series that are specific to their own countries.

6. When they have finished, ask each student to write a few sentences about the way things used to be for their partner as a child, and the ways in which they are different now. For example:
Julio used to have long blond hair but he didn't use to have a moustache.

ANSWERS
What games did you use to play?
What TV series did you use to watch?
What hobbies did you use to have?
What pets did you use to have?
What music did you use to like?
What clothes did you use to wear?
What did you use to look like?
What did you use to be like?
What tech did you use to use?
What food did you use to hate?
What did you use to be frightened of?
What ambitions did you use to have?

11 When in Rome

While he was working in San Francisco, Mr Scotti received an invitation to visit his relatives in Italy.

As soon as he had a free moment, he went online and booked a flight for the following week.

As he set off on his journey he was feeling excited and was already looking forward to some home cooking.

When the plane landed in New York, Mr Scotti didn't take the connecting flight because he thought they were in Italy.

He went to the exit, but there was nobody there to meet him. He asked a police officer, in Italian, for directions to the city centre.

The police officer was from Naples so he answered fluently in the same language.

As Mr Scotti was travelling to the city centre, he looked around and noticed how sad it was that Rome

was as modern as any American city now. Also, the place was full of American tourists!

After walking around for a while, he asked another police officer for directions.

He was amazed that she didn't understand Italian.

When the police officer told him he was in New York, Mr Scotti didn't believe her.

The police officer offered to take him back to the airport, and as soon as they set off

in the police car, she put the siren on and started driving very fast.

'There', said Mr Scotti, 'now I know I'm in Italy because that's how we drive.'

11 When in Rome

ACTIVITY
Whole class: speaking, reading, writing

AIM
To put a story in the correct order by saying and listening to sentences
To write the story down in a group dictation

GRAMMAR AND FUNCTIONS
Telling a story: *when*, *as soon as*, *as*, *while*

When and *as soon as* + past simple for actions which happen one after the other

When, *as* and *while* + past continuous for longer actions

VOCABULARY
A journey

TIME
45 minutes

PREPARATION
Make one copy of the worksheet for each group of 14 students. Cut out the sentences (or parts of sentences) into cards as indicated.
Have one copy of the complete story to hand to display to students at the end of the activity.

PROCEDURE
1. Tell students that they are going to read a story about Mr Scotti, an Italian living in America, but that the story is in 14 parts which aren't in order. They will have to put the sentences of the story in the correct order.

2. Divide students into groups of 14 and give each group a set of cut-up cards, shuffled into random order. If the number of students in the class is not an exact multiple of 14, give one part of the story to a pair of students.

3. In their groups, each student takes one part of the story. If you have fewer than 14 students in the class or group, distribute the parts yourself and give some students two consecutive parts of the story. If you have students of mixed abilities, give shorter sentences to less confident students.

4. Tell students that they are responsible for their own sentence for the rest of the activity. Ask them to read it and make sure they understand it.

5. Ask students to practise saying their own sentence aloud and to memorise it. Go round helping them individually with pronunciation problems.

6. When students have memorised their own sentence, tell them to stand up in their groups and to form a line in the order of the story by saying their sentences aloud. This stage of the activity may seem rather chaotic at first, but try not to intervene as one of the aims of this activity is for students to repeat their sentence several times and listen to other students' sentences carefully.

7. When the story is in the correct order, ask students to sit down in their groups and get ready to write the story.

8. Explain that each student is going to write the whole story. Each student dictates their own sentence to the rest of the group and answers questions about the spelling and punctuation of their sentence.

9. Ask the student with the first line to read it out for the rest of the group to write down. Students then take it in turns to read out their sentences in order for the rest of the group to write them down.

10. When everybody has written down the complete story, give out copies of the complete worksheet and display it to the class so that students can correct their own work.

FOLLOW-UP
Ask the class if they can think of any funny travel stories that have happened to them or someone they know.

12 Really?!

1 fold **2** fold **3**

_____ ,	who likes _____ ,	didn't use to _____
_____ ,	who hates _____ ,	_____ last night.
_____ ,	who's got _____ ,	_____ every day.
_____ ,	who looks like _____ ,	feels _____
_____ ,	who enjoys _____ ,	would like to _____
_____ ,	who plays _____ ,	is good at _____
_____ ,	who's wearing _____ ,	often _____
_____ ,	who never _____ ,	sings _____
_____ ,	who was born _____ ,	is going to _____
_____ ,	who lives _____ ,	has never _____
_____ ,	who's working _____ ,	never _____
_____ ,	who had _____ ,	_____ once a week.
_____ ,	who's _____ ,	likes listening to _____
_____ ,	who doesn't like _____ ,	used to _____

12 Really?!

ACTIVITY
Pairwork: writing, speaking

AIM
To write imaginary information about people by completing unfinished sentences

GRAMMAR AND FUNCTIONS
Non-defining relative clauses with *who* for giving additional information about people

VOCABULARY
General

TIME
20–30 minutes

PREPARATION
Make one copy of the worksheet for each student in the class.

PROCEDURE
1. If there are more than 14 students in the class, divide them into groups.

2. Give one copy of the worksheet to each student in the class.

3. Ask each student to write down the names of everybody in the class or group, in random order, in column 1 of their worksheet. If there are fewer than 14 students in the class they should write some names twice.

4. When they have done that, ask students to fold their piece of paper as indicated so that columns 1 and 3 are hidden and only column 2 is visible. They should give it to the student on their left.

5. Ask students to complete the first relative clause in column 2 in any way they like. For example:

… who likes sleeping

… who likes chocolate

Encourage students to be as imaginative or as amusing as they like.

6. When they have done that, ask students to give the paper to the student on their left. You may need to give a 30-second time limit for completing each clause in order to avoid some students finishing before others.

7. Now ask students to complete the next clause in column 2 on the piece of paper they have received and then give it to the student on their left.

8. Repeat the activity until all the clauses in column 2 have been completed.

9. Now ask students to turn their piece of paper over so that only column 3 is visible. They should complete the first verb phrase in column 3 in any way they like. For example:

… didn't use to speak English.

… didn't use to have a moustache.

… didn't use to be frightened of flying.

10. When they have done that, ask students to give the paper to the student on their left and continue as before until all the phrases have been completed.

11. Tell students to open out the completed worksheet they have received and to read the sentences on their piece of paper.

12. If there are any words or phrases that the students do not understand or think are incorrect, tell them to find the student who wrote them and ask them to explain or correct the word or phrase.

13. Ask each student to read out any sentences which are true or particularly amusing.

14. Display the sentences so that students can read them.

13 Problems, problems, problems

COMPLAINT soup cold	**COMPLAINT** wrong change	**COMPLAINT** heating in hotel room not working
REQUEST another bowl	**REQUEST** €2 more	**REQUEST** repair it
COMPLAINT you're on mute	**COMPLAINT** can't hear you	**COMPLAINT** bought a book - pages missing
REQUEST unmute	**REQUEST** turn on your microphone	**REQUEST** another one
COMPLAINT ordered coffee, not tea	**COMPLAINT** meeting room too small	**COMPLAINT** bought a jumper - hole in it
REQUEST a cup of coffee	**REQUEST** a bigger one	**REQUEST** a new one
COMPLAINT bought a laptop - doesn't work	**COMPLAINT** room too hot	**COMPLAINT** driving too fast
REQUEST money back	**REQUEST** open a window	**REQUEST** slow down

13 Problems, problems, problems

ACTIVITY
Whole class: speaking
Mill drill. See the front of the book for detailed instructions and advice on using mill drills.

AIM
To speak to as many partners as possible; making complaints, apologising and making requests

GRAMMAR AND FUNCTIONS
Complaining: *I'm sorry ..., I'm afraid ...*
Apologising
Responding to apologies
Making requests

VOCABULARY
General

TIME
15 to 20 minutes

PREPARATION
Make one copy of the worksheet for each group of up to 12 students. Cut the worksheet up into cards as indicated so that students have one card each. You will need to keep one card for yourself to demonstrate the activity.

PROCEDURE
1. If there are more than 12 students in the class, divide them into groups. Give one card to each student and keep one for yourself.

2. Tell students that they are going to make complaints and requests using the words and pictures on their cards as prompts. Before they start the activity, ask each student to look at their own card and to write on the other side who they are complaining to and where they are. Tell the students to ask you if they are not sure what the illustration on their card shows.
For example: Waiter, in a restaurant

3. Write example dialogues on the board indicating the language the students should use. Explain that Student A's complaint and request will depend on the words and picture on their

card and that Student B's response will vary slightly depending on the situation as written on the other side of the card.

For example:
Student A: *Excuse me! I'm afraid my soup is cold.*
Student B: *I'm very sorry.*
Student A: *That's all right but could you bring me another bowl please?*

Student B: *I'm sorry but you've given me the wrong change.*
Student A: *I'm really sorry.*
Student B: *That's OK but would you mind giving me €2 more?*

4. Demonstrate the activity with individual students. Tell students to hold their cards so the picture is facing them and the side they have written on is facing their partner. Ask several pairs of students to demonstrate the activity to the whole class, using their cards as prompts.

5. Now ask students to go round the class complaining, apologising and making requests with as many different partners as possible, using their cards as prompts. In this part of the activity, students practise making the same complaint and request several times.

6. When the students have finished, ask them to exchange cards and to go round the class again, this time holding their cards the other way round so the word and picture prompt is facing their partner. Students take it in turns to make complaints and requests using the prompts on their partner's cards. In this part of the activity, students make different complaints and requests each time they change partner.

7. Students continue in this way until they have spoken to as many different partners as possible.

14 Dominoes

exhausted	tasty	delicious	angry	furious	annoying
infuriating	frightening	terrifying	hot	boiling	funny
hilarious	hungry	starving	surprised	astonished	interesting
fascinating	silly	ridiculous	big	huge	good
excellent	cold	freezing	clever	brilliant	wet
soaked	small	tiny	pleased	delighted	pretty
gorgeous	difficult	impossible	old	ancient	sad
miserable	horrible	disgusting	crowded	packed	quiet
silent	exciting	thrilling	bad	awful	clean
spotless	important	essential	valuable	precious	tired

14 Dominoes

ACTIVITY
Groupwork: speaking

AIM
To play a game of dominoes matching adjectives and their strong equivalents

GRAMMAR AND FUNCTIONS
Adjectives

VOCABULARY
Base and strong adjectives, for example:
angry – furious, cold – freezing

TIME
20 to 30 minutes

PREPARATION
Make one copy of the worksheet for every four or five students in the class and cut out all the cards as indicated. You may wish to stick the worksheet onto card before cutting it up.

PROCEDURE
1. Explain to students that they are going to play a game of dominoes, matching adjectives and their strong equivalents, for example, *angry – furious*. The object of the game is for students to get rid of all their dominoes.

2. Ask students to work in groups of four or five and give each group of students a set of dominoes. Ask one student in each group to deal out five dominoes to each person and to leave the rest in a pile, face down.

3. Before they start, explain how to play using the instructions below. If you wish, you can give a copy of these instructions to each group or display them to the class.

4. Play the game. While they are playing, go round to each group and check any queries about meaning or pronunciation.

5. When students have finished the game they can reshuffle and play another round.

HOW TO PLAY THE GAME
1. Player A puts down one of their dominoes face up.

2. The player on their left (Player B) must then put down one of their dominoes, making sure that one of the words on their domino matches one of the words on either side of Player A's domino. Player B puts their domino so the matching words touch.

For example:
Domino A: *exhausted / tasty*
Domino B: either *tired* or *delicious*

| precious / tired | exhausted / tasty | delicious / angry |

3. If a player cannot put down one of their dominoes, they take a domino from the top of the pile and put it down if they can.

4. The winner is the first player to get rid of all their dominoes.

ANSWERS

tasty – delicious	small – tiny
angry – furious	pleased – delighted
annoying – infuriating	pretty – gorgeous
frightening – terrifying	difficult – impossible
hot – boiling	old – ancient
funny – hilarious	sad – miserable
hungry – starving	horrible – disgusting
surprised – astonished	crowded – packed
interesting – fascinating	quiet – silent
silly – ridiculous	exciting – thrilling
big – huge	bad – awful
good – excellent	clean – spotless
cold – freezing	important – essential
clever – brilliant	valuable – precious
wet – soaked	tired – exhausted

15 Around the world

First throw ⟶

	1	2	3	4	5
1	do a tour of street food in Mumbai, India	go walking in the Himalayas, Nepal	ride a horse to the Lost City of Petra in Jordan	take a road trip in California, USA	watch a surfing competition in Peniche, Portugal
2	watch whales near Vancouver, Canada	eat cakes in Vienna, Austria	sleep under the stars in the Sahara desert in Morocco	have breakfast in the park in Cairo, Egypt	visit the Old Town of Warsaw, Poland
3	go to a jazz club in Rio, Brazil	listen to a local band in Nairobi, Kenya	go on a tour of street art in Bangkok, Thailand	have a drink in a rooftop bar in Hong Kong	do yoga in the park in Barcelona, Spain
4	go bird-watching in Reykjavik, Iceland	drink Turkish coffee in Istanbul, Turkey	take photos of temples in Kyoto, Japan	walk along the Great Wall of China	climb the Empire State Building in New York, US
5	watch a football match in Milan, Italy	see an opera in Buenos Aires, Argentina	swim under waterfalls near Darwin, Australia	work on a sheep farm in Christchurch, New Zealand	have a sauna in Helsinki, Finland

Second throw ↓

15 Around the world

ACTIVITY
Pairwork and groupwork: speaking, writing

AIM
To talk about things you've done and things you haven't done by playing a card game

GRAMMAR AND FUNCTIONS
Present perfect simple: *already*, *yet*, *still*

VOCABULARY
Leisure activities, cities and countries

TIME
35 to 45 minutes

PREPARATION
- Make one copy of the complete worksheet for each pair of students in the class.
- Make one copy of the worksheet for each group of four to six students and cut it into destination cards.
- Provide dice for each group of students.

PROCEDURE
1. Ask students to work in groups of four or six and to work with a partner in their group.

2. Give one set of destination cards and a dice to each group. Give one copy of the destination sheet to each pair of students. Explain that the object of the game is to go to as many destinations as possible in ten minutes.

3. Before students start playing the game, explain how to play using the instructions opposite.

4. Students are ready to play the game. Start the timer.

5. After ten minutes, ask students to turn their destination sheets over so that they are face down.

6. Give them five minutes to remember and write down a) the places they have crossed off and the activities they have done there and b) the places they haven't visited yet.

7. After five minutes, ask students to stay in their groups and check one another's answers. They get one point for each place and two points for each activity they have remembered correctly. Encourage students to use the present perfect when they read out their answers. For example, *We've done a tour of street food in Mumbai, we've taken a road trip in California, we've eaten cakes in Vienna, but we haven't ridden a horse to the Lost City of Petra and we haven't watched a surfing competition in Portugal yet.*

8. Students can now continue playing the game until the first pair of students has crossed off all the places on their destinations sheet.

HOW TO PLAY THE GAME
1. Work with a partner in your group. Each pair has one destinations sheet and each group has one set of destination cards and a dice.

2. Each pair takes four destination cards. These are the places you've already been to and you should cross them off on the destinations sheet.

3. Each pair throws the dice and the pair which throws the highest number starts the game.

4. Pairs take it in turns to throw the dice twice to find their next destination. The first number they throw refers to the numbers across the top of the destinations sheet and the second number refers to the line of numbers down the side. For example, if the players throw a 2 and then a 4, they land on 'drink Turkish coffee in Istanbul, Turkey'. They should then cross this off on their destinations sheet to show that they have been there and done the activity.

5. If players land on a place they've already been to and crossed out, they miss their turn. If they throw a six, they throw the dice again.

6. The game continues for ten minutes. Then everyone must stop playing and listen to the teacher's instructions.

16 How long ...?

Who's been learning English the longest? Find out.

Who's been playing their favourite sport the longest? Find out.

 Who's known their oldest friend the longest? Find out.

Who's had their pet the longest? Find out.

Who's been doing their hobby the longest? Find out.

Who's been going to the same hairdresser the longest? Find out.

 Who's been living in the same place the longest? Find out.

Who's been wearing the same watch the longest? Find out.

Who's been driving the same car or riding the same bicycle or motor bike the longest? Find out.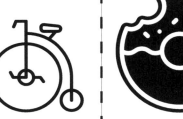

 Who's had the same bad habit the longest? Find out.

 Who's known you the longest in the group? Find out.

Who's had their favourite pair of jeans the longest? Find out.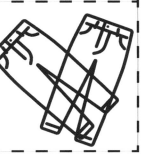

16 How long ...?

ACTIVITY
Whole class: speaking

AIM
To find out how long people have been doing things by asking and answering questions

GRAMMAR AND FUNCTIONS
Present perfect simple or continuous for asking and saying how long

VOCABULARY
General

TIME
15 to 20 minutes

PREPARATION
Make one copy of the worksheet for each group of up to 12 students. Cut the cards out as indicated.

PROCEDURE
1. If there are more than 12 students in the class, divide them into groups. Give one card to each student in the class.

2. Tell students that they are responsible for finding the answer to the question on their own card by speaking to everybody in their group. Make sure they know how to formulate their question correctly.

3. Now ask students to go round the class or group, asking and answering questions. Tell them that they can make notes on the back of their card if necessary.

4. When they have spoken to everybody in the class or group, students should sit down and work out the answer to their question.

5. Now ask students to take it in turns to report back to the class or group on the information they have found out.

FOLLOW-UP
Ask students to stay in their groups and to write a summary of the information they have gathered to be displayed to the class.

17 Comparisons

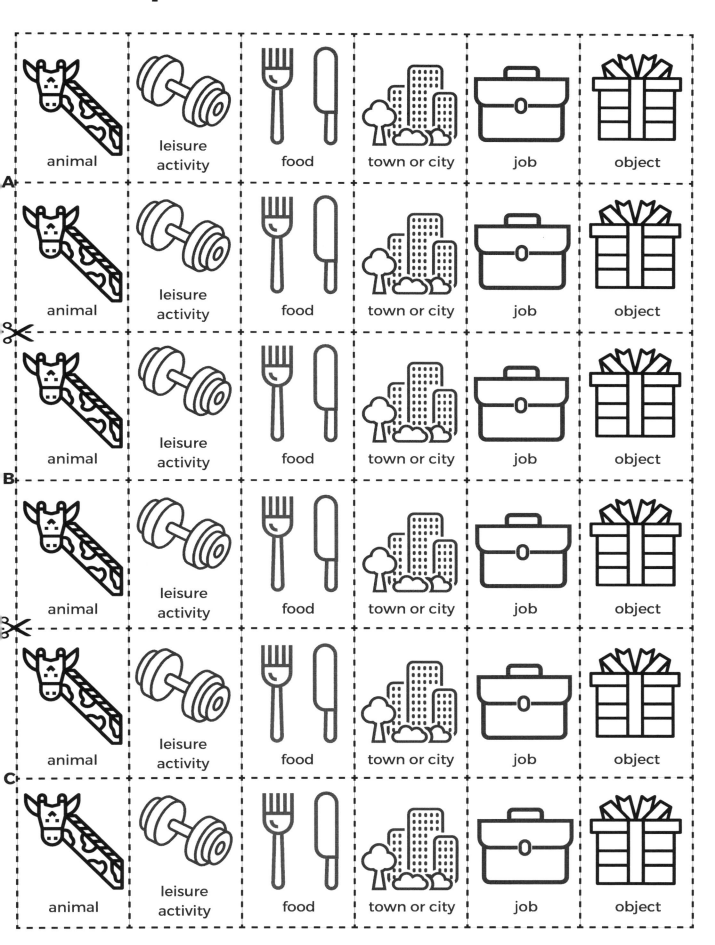

A

| animal | leisure activity | food | town or city | job | object |

| animal | leisure activity | food | town or city | job | object |

B

| animal | leisure activity | food | town or city | job | object |

| animal | leisure activity | food | town or city | job | object |

C

| animal | leisure activity | food | town or city | job | object |

| animal | leisure activity | food | town or city | job | object |

17 Comparisons

ACTIVITY
Groupwork: speaking

AIM
To make comparisons using cards

GRAMMAR AND FUNCTIONS
Making comparisons:
comparative adjective + *than*
more/less + comparative adjective + *than*
more + countable/uncountable noun + *than*
fewer + plural countable noun + *than*
less + uncountable noun + *than*
as much + uncountable noun + *as*
as many + plural countable noun + *as*
as + adjective + *as*

VOCABULARY
General

TIME
15 to 20 minutes

PREPARATION
Make one copy of the worksheet for each group of three students. Cut the worksheets into sections A, B and C. Cut each section into cards as shown.

PROCEDURE
1. Ask students to work in groups of three, Student A, B and C, and give a set of A cards to each Student A, a set of B cards to each Student B and a set of C cards to each Student C.

2. Ask students to write one word belonging to the category on the back of each card, for example: *animal: lion, leisure activity: reading.*

3. Next, groups of three should shuffle their cards together and spread them on the table with the category headings facing up, and the words they have written on the back facing down.

4. In groups, students take it in turns to turn over two cards of the same category and make a comparison between the words they have turned over. For example, if the words are lion and frog:
A lion is bigger than a frog.
A lion is more dangerous than a frog.
A frog can swim better than a lion.
A frog is not as beautiful as a lion.

If a student turns over two identical words, they should make a superlative sentence. For example, if both words are *lion*:
The lion is the most beautiful animal in Africa.

5. When a student has finished their sentence and the other students in the group agree it is correct, the student who made the sentence picks up the two cards and keeps them.

6. If a student cannot think of a sentence, they miss a turn. If a student makes a sentence which is grammatically incorrect or which does not make sense, the rest of the group can challenge it. If the student can explain the sentence to the satisfaction of the rest of the group, the student can keep the cards. If not, they should turn them over and leave them on the table.

7. Continue the activity until all the cards have been used. The student with the most cards at the end of the activity is the winner.

OPTION
Follow Procedure points 1 and 2 as above.

3. Ask students to put their words into six piles according to the categories.

4. Choose a category. Students have to arrange the words they have written in that category in order according to certain criteria. For example:
Animals from most to least dangerous.
Leisure activities from most to least expensive.

18 Describing objects - cards

comfortable	twentieth century	black	Mexican	glass	made from recycled material
smart	new	brown	Italian	china	with diamonds
beautiful	old	blue	Swiss	woollen	with a silver strap
pretty	small	yellow	Chinese	leather	with gold buttons
nice	big	red	Japanese	gold	with flowers on it
lovely	large	white	French	silver	with my initials on it

18 Describing objects

ACTIVITY
Groupwork: speaking

AIM
To play a board game by using adjectives in the correct order when describing objects

GRAMMAR AND FUNCTIONS
Order of adjectives and phrases for describing objects

VOCABULARY
Adjectives for describing opinion, size, age, shape, colour, origin and material

TIME
30 minutes

PREPARATION
- Make one copy of the Game Board for every three to four students in the class.
- Make two copies of the Cards sheet for every three to four students in the class and cut them up as indicated.
- Make one copy of the How To Play The Game instructions for each group.
- Provide counters and dice for each group.

PROCEDURE
1. Ask students to work in groups of three or four. Give one game board, two sets of cards (mixed up), How To Play instructions, counters and dice to each group.

2. Before students start playing, explain how to play using the instructions.

3. Demonstrate with an example: if a student lands on *jumper* and they have the following cards: *lovely, nice, white, leather, Italian* and *with flowers on it*, they can put down *lovely, white, Italian* and *with flowers on it*, or *nice, white, Italian* and *with flowers on it*. They can't use *leather* because a jumper is made of wool, and they can't use *lovely* and *nice* together.

4. Students are ready to play the game. While they are playing, go round to each group and answer questions and offer help.

18 Describing objects - game board

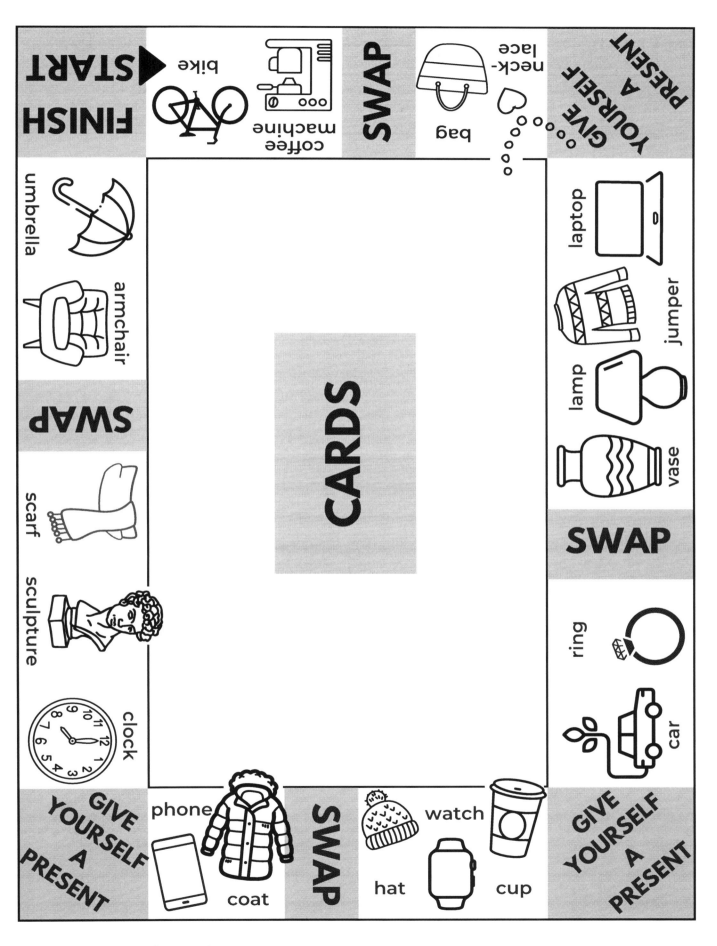

18 Describing objects

HOW TO PLAY THE GAME

1. Put the game board in the middle of the table and give six cards to each player. Place the remaining cards face down in the space provided on the board.

2. All the players put their counters on the square marked START and throw the dice. The first player to throw a six starts the game.

3. Player 1 throws the dice and moves their counter along the board according to the number on the dice.

4. Player 1 then reads the word on the square they have landed on and puts down as many of their cards that could be used to describe the word, making sure they are in the correct order. Note that students can describe ANY watch, car, etc., not just the one on the board.

5. If a group thinks that an adjective/phrase is in the wrong position or that it is not appropriate, they can reject it.

6. When a player has used their cards to the satisfaction of the other players, they keep the cards they have used in a pile next to them and then pick up the same number of new cards from the pile in the middle of the board.

7. If a player lands on a square marked SWAP, they can exchange any of the cards in their hand by putting them at the bottom of the pile in the middle of the board and taking the same number from the top of the pile.

8. If a player lands on a square marked GIVE YOURSELF A PRESENT, they can invent an object and describe it using as many of their cards as they like and then continue as in point 5 and 6 above.

The game continues until the first player reaches the square marked FINISH or all the cards have been used up. The winner is the player with the most cards in their pile.

19 What's in your wardrobe?

1 What kind of clothes do you like?

_____

_____

2 What do you wear to school / work / college?

_____

_____

3 Do you know anyone who makes their own clothes?

_____

_____

4 What do you do with your old clothes?

_____

_____

5 Describe your favourite item of clothing.

_____

_____

6 Have you ever bought second-hand clothes?

_____

_____

7 What matters most when you buy new clothes?
a) price   b) fashion
c) eco-friendly materials

_____

_____

8 Do you ever swap clothes with your friends?

_____

_____

9 Do you prefer to buy clothes online or in shops?

_____

_____

10 What do you wear for special occasions?

_____

_____

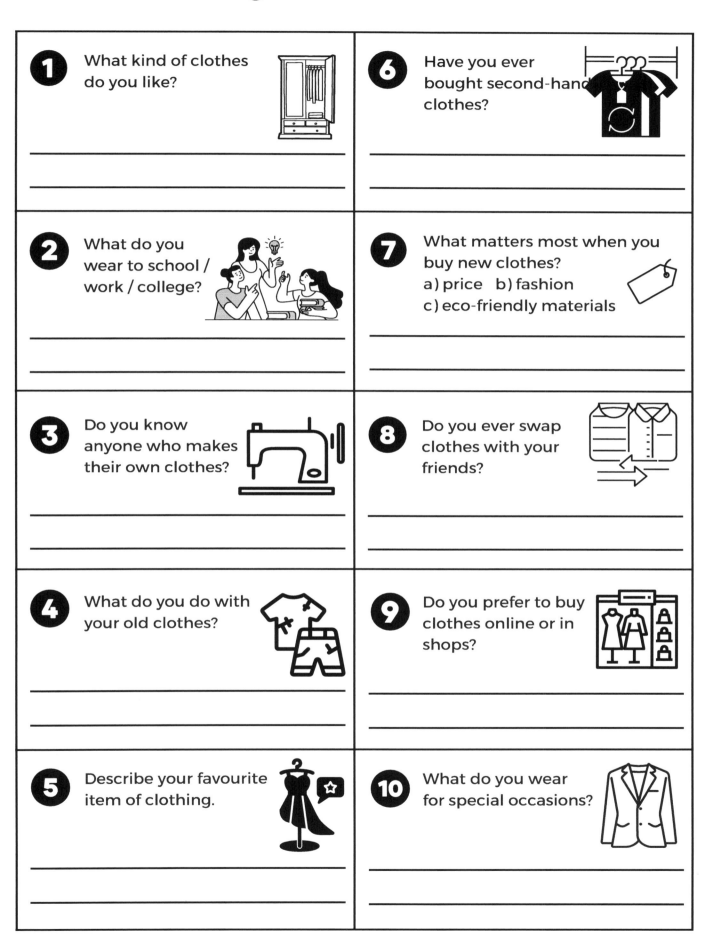

19 What's in your wardrobe?

ACTIVITY
Pairwork: speaking, writing
Questionnaire

AIM
To ask and answer questions about your clothes

GRAMMAR AND FUNCTIONS
Talking about your clothes

VOCABULARY
Clothes

TIME
20 to 30 minutes

PREPARATION
Make one copy of the worksheet for each student in the class.

PROCEDURE
1. Ask students to work in pairs. Give one copy of the worksheet to each student in the class.

2. Tell students that they are going to interview one another using the questionnaire on the worksheet but that they have got a few moments to think about their own answers first. Students check that they know the vocabulary on the worksheet, and think about their answers. They shouldn't write their answers down yet.

3. When they are ready, ask students to interview one another and to make notes of their partner's answers in the spaces provided on the questionnaire. They should not write their partner's name on the questionnaire.

4. When students have finished interviewing one another in pairs, take the completed questionnaires in and mix them up.

5. Now give one completed worksheet to each student in the class so that they have a questionnaire which is neither their own nor the one they completed for their partner.

6. Ask students to read the answers on the questionnaire they have been given, and to guess who it belongs to. As they read, they should correct any mistakes they find.

7. Students say whether they guessed whose questionnaire they had correctly.

OPTION
After Procedure point 3, simply ask students to report back to the class on anything surprising they have found out about their partner during the activity.

© ELT Teacher 2 Writer. Written by Sue Kay.

20 Predict your future

	I'm sure I will	I probably will	I might	I probably won't	I definitely won't
In the next five years ... move house set up my own company					
Before your next birthday ... get fitter take an exam					
In the next ten years ... have children learn a new skill					
In the next six months ... have a party paint a picture					
This week ... give somebody flowers try a new recipe					
Today ... go for a run send an email					
In your life ... become famous invent something					
This year ... travel by train give a presentation					
This month ... do something for charity win the lottery					
In the next few days ... go to a restaurant make new friends					
Before you die ... live in another country write a book					
Tomorrow ... get up early do some gardening					

20 Predict your future

ACTIVITY
Whole class: speaking, writing

AIM
To ask and answer questions about the future and to create a group poster

GRAMMAR AND FUNCTIONS
Making predictions, certainty, probability, possibility
certain: *I'm sure I will, I definitely won't*
probable: *I probably will/won't*
possible: *I might*

VOCABULARY
Everyday activities

TIME
20 minutes

PREPARATION
Make one copy of the worksheet for each group of up to 12 students and cut them into cards as indicated.

PROCEDURE
1. If there are more than 12 students in the class, divide them into groups.

2. Give one card to each student in the class and tell them that they are going to ask and answer questions about the future. Explain that each student is responsible for finding out the information on their own card by speaking to everybody in the class or group.

3. Before they start the activity, make sure everybody knows how to ask the question they need to ask in order to find out the information on their card. Write these sentences on the board:

I'm sure I will.
I probably will.
I might.
I probably won't.
I definitely won't.

Elicit questions and answers. For example:

Student A: *Do you think you'll move house in the next five years?*
Student B: (choosing one of the possible answers) *No, I probably won't.*

Put a tick next to *I probably won't.*

Student B: *Do you think you'll get fitter before your next birthday?*
Student A: *I might.*

Put a tick next to *I might.*

4. Now ask students to go round the class or group, asking and answering their questions and putting a tick for each answer in the relevant column on their card.

5. When they have spoken to everybody in the class or group, ask them to work with two or three other students in their group and to write down some of the information they have gathered either on a poster or on a shared document. For example:

In our group nobody thinks they will move house in the next five years.
Only one person thinks they will get fitter before their next birthday.

21 Can you do it?

Find out how many people ...

- can wake up on time without an alarm.
- can fall asleep in a chair.
- can be cheerful before 9 o'clock in the morning.

Find out how many people ...

- can spell *beautiful*.
- can spell *through*.
- can spell *laugh*.

Find out how many people ...

- can name three Chinese cities.
- can see three things beginning with 's'.
- can see three things made of wood.

Find out how many people ...

- can do homework and listen to music at the same time.
- can type without looking at their fingers.
- can write neatly with both hands.

Find out how many people ...

- can remember what they had for lunch yesterday.
- can remember what they did on their last birthday.
- can remember the name of the first teacher they had.

Find out how many people ...

- can say *hello* in four languages.
- can see the same film twice without getting bored.
- can listen to a podcast and do exercise at the same time.

Find out how many people ...

- can name three animals in danger.
- can draw a recycling symbol.
- can spell *environment*.

Find out how many people ...

- can name five vegetables.
- can name four types of music.
- can think of three verbs beginning with 'r'.

21 Can you do it?

ACTIVITY
Groupwork: speaking

AIM
To find out what people can do by asking and answering questions

GRAMMAR AND FUNCTIONS
Can to talk about general ability in the present

VOCABULARY
General

TIME
20 to 30 minutes

PREPARATION
Make one copy of the worksheet for each group of up to eight students. Cut the cards up as indicated.

PROCEDURE
1. If there are more than eight students in the class, divide them into groups. Give one card to each student in the class.

2. Ask students to read through their card and check they know the meanings of all the phrases. Explain any new words.

3. Tell students that they are responsible for finding out the information on their own card by speaking to everybody in the class or group.

4. Now ask students to go round the class or group asking and answering questions. Tell them to put a tick next to a sentence each time somebody answers *Yes, I can* or succeeds in doing the task.

5. When they have spoken to everybody in the class or group, students should sit down in their groups and take it in turns to talk about the information they have found out.

22 It says in the contract ...

Contract for students

Class times

Students should be in the classroom five minutes before the teacher and they mustn't leave before the lesson has ended. Students who arrive late should not expect their teacher to believe their excuses.

Behaviour in class

Students should be polite to one another and the teacher.

Students should keep their phones on silent, but if they have to send a text, they shouldn't disturb the rest of the class.

Students are not supposed to chew gum, but if it helps their pronunciation, it's ok.

Homework

Students mustn't use the following excuses if they haven't done their homework: 'The dog ate it' or 'My computer got a virus and deleted all my files'.

Presents

Students should give their teacher a present at the end of each term.

I agree to respect the rules and obligations above.

Signed ....

Contract for teachers

_____

_____

_____

_____

_____

_____

_____

_____

_____

_____

I agree to respect the rules and obligations above.

Signed ....

22 It says in the contract ...

ACTIVITY
Groupwork: reading, speaking, writing

AIM
To write an imaginary contract for teachers

GRAMMAR AND FUNCTIONS
Modal verbs:
should, must for giving advice
have to, must, mustn't for obligation
don't have to for lack of obligation
be supposed to to talk about what people are
expected to do because of a rule or tradition

VOCABULARY
School rules

TIME
20 to 30 minutes

PREPARATION
Make one copy of the worksheet for each group
of three students in the class.

PROCEDURE
1. Ask students to call out any school rules they
can think of.

2. Now ask them to work in groups of three. Give
one copy of the worksheet to each group of
students and ask them if any of the rules they
have thought of are mentioned in the 'Contract for
students'. Draw their attention to the modal verbs
that are used in the contract and make sure they
understand how to use them.

3. Tell students that they are going to write a
'Contract for teachers' including the rules and
regulations they think teachers should follow.
Each group should appoint a secretary to do the
writing. Encourage students to be as imaginative
or as amusing as they like, and to use the target
language. While they are doing this, go round the
class checking that they are using the modal verbs
correctly.

4. Display the 'Contracts for teachers' for other
students to read and compare with their own.

23 Film review

Title of the film _____

Type of film _____

The main actors _____

What it's about _____

_____

What you thought of it _____

_____

23 Film review

ACTIVITY
Groupwork: speaking, writing

AIM
To write reviews of imaginary films by looking at pictures which could be film posters

GRAMMAR AND FUNCTIONS
Adjectives and adverbs: *amazing – amazingly, beautiful – beautifully, remarkable – remarkably, extraordinary – extraordinarily,* etc.

Giving opinions:

I thought it was really good/funny.

I found it interesting/boring.

I've never seen such a terrible/brilliant film.

It's well/not worth seeing.

As far as I'm concerned, it's the best/worst film I've ever seen.

Emphasising: *absolutely, extremely, really, particularly*

VOCABULARY
Types of film, parts of a film, adjectives to describe a film

TIME
45 minutes

PREPARATION
- Make one copy of the worksheet and cut off the film review section as indicated.
- Make one copy of the pictures, cut them out and stick each picture in the middle of a blank piece of A4 or A3 paper.
- Make one copy of the pictures for each group of three students in the class. Don't cut the pictures up.
- Make two copies of the film review chart for each group of three students.

PROCEDURE
1. Ask students to think about what makes a good film and to call out their ideas.

2. Divide students into six groups and tell them that they are going to look at some film posters. Give one picture on a blank piece of paper to each group and ask them to write words or expressions which they associate with the picture or the type of film it illustrates on the space around the picture. Words may include adjectives (*funny, scary,* etc.), aspects of the plot (*falling in love, a happy ending, a murder,* etc.), props (*guns, torch, aliens,* etc.), scenery (*a planet far from earth, downtown New York, the Swiss mountains*) or costumes (*police uniforms, brightly coloured dresses, spacesuit,* etc.).

3. After three minutes, ask students to give their picture, with the words and expressions written around it, to the group of students on their left. Tell them that they have two minutes to read what the other group has written and add words and expressions of their own.

4. Continue like this until each group has seen each picture. While they are doing this part of the activity, go round to each group, answering questions and offering help. Display the completed pictures round the class so that students can refer to them if necessary.

5. Now ask students to work in groups of three. Give one copy of the pictures and two copies of the film review section of the worksheet to each group of students.

6. Ask each group to choose two of the pictures and write reviews of the films they illustrate by inventing details to complete the film review. Encourage students to be as imaginative or amusing as they like.

7. When they have finished, ask students to read out their reviews without showing the corresponding pictures. The rest of the class should guess which picture they refer to.

FOLLOW-UP
Each group chooses one film and writes the plot – the class awards an Oscar for the best one.

24 My life as an animal

	the place where you live	something you do well
	something nice you hope to do in the next few days	
something you do badly		
	something you didn't enjoy doing in the last few days	something you usually do after supper
your favourite place		your best characteristics

24 My life as an animal

ACTIVITY
Pairwork: writing, speaking

AIM
To pretend you're an animal and to give personal information as if you were that animal
To guess what animal other people are pretending to be

GRAMMAR AND FUNCTIONS
Position of adverbs and adverb phrases
Adverbs of manner: *well, badly*
Adverb phrases of time: *in the last/next few days*; *after supper*

VOCABULARY
Animals and the way they live their lives

TIME
15 to 20 minutes

PREPARATION
Make one copy of the worksheet for each student in the class.

PROCEDURE
1. Tell students that you're going to talk to them from the point of view of an animal and that they should guess, from the information you give them, what the animal is. For example:
I live in Asia.
I fight well but I swim badly.
I hope to kill a deer and eat some of my favourite meat in the next few days.
I didn't enjoy seeing humans with guns in the last few days.
I usually sleep after supper.
My favourite place is the rainforest.
I'm beautiful, strong and dangerous.
Answer: *tiger*

2. Give a copy of the worksheet to each student in the class.

3. Tell them to imagine that they are an animal and to write information on their worksheet from the animal's point of view.

4. Ask students to work in pairs and take it in turns to read out their information to their partner. They must guess what their partner's animal is.

5. Tell students to find a new partner and repeat procedure point 4.

FOLLOW-UP
1. Give students another copy of the worksheet and ask them to fill it in with information about themselves without writing their names.

2. When they have done that, take the worksheets in, mix them up and display them so that students can read them and guess who wrote them.

25 Love is ...

2. One should always be in love. That is the reason one should never marry.
Oscar Wilde

1. True love is like ghosts, which everyone talks about and few have seen.
Francois de la Rochefoucauld

3. I really love the togetherness in baseball. That's a real true love.
Billy Martin

4. True love lasts forever.
Joseph B. Wirthlin

5. Life without love is a tree without blossoms or fruit.
Khahil Gibran

6. Love means having to say you're sorry every fifteen minutes.
John Lennon

7. Life is a game and true love is a trophy.
Rufus Wainwright

8. Where there is love there is life.
Mahatma Gandhi

9. Love conquers all things, except poverty and toothache.
Mae West

10. He who falls in love with himself will have no rivals.
Benjamin Franklin

11. True love comes quietly, without banners or flashing lights.
Erich Segal

12. Love is pure and true, love knows no gender.
Tori Spelling

13. All you need is love.
The Beatles

14. The course of true love never did run smooth.
William Shakespeare

Cynical	Romantic	Realistic

25 Love is ...

ACTIVITY
Pairwork: speaking

AIM
To categorise quotes about love and to discuss
attitudes to being in love

GRAMMAR AND FUNCTIONS
Reported speech
Said (that) + clause

VOCABULARY
Love and relationships

TIME
20 to 30 minutes

PREPARATION
Make one copy of the worksheet for each pair of
students in the class.

PROCEDURE
1. Ask students to suggest different ways of
completing the sentence *Love is ...* and write
some of them on the board. Ask students to put
these definitions into the categories *cynical*,
romantic or *realistic*. Ensure students understand
cynical (negative, distrusting, always assuming a
bad outcome). Give a definition in students' L1 if
appropriate.

2. Now ask students to work in pairs. Give one
copy of the worksheet to each pair.

3. Ask them to decide which category the
definitions of love fall into and then to write the
numbers corresponding to the definitions under
the relevant headings.

4. When they have done that, students should add
one definition of their own to each category.

5. Ask students to compare worksheets with
another pair of students and notice any
differences. They should discuss the way they
have categorised the definitions.

6. Ask students to report any differences in
opinion to the class. Encourage them to use the
target language, for example:
*Monica and Akemi said that 'Love means having
to say you're sorry every fifteen minutes' was
realistic, but we thought it was cynical.*

SUGGESTED ANSWERS
Cynical
1. True love is like ghosts, which everyone talks
about and few have seen.
2. One should always be in love. That is the
reason one should never marry.
6. Love means having to say you're sorry every
fifteen minutes.
10. He who falls in love with himself will have
no rivals.

Romantic
4. True love lasts forever.
5. Life without love is a tree without blossoms or
fruit.
7. Life is a game and true love is a trophy.
13. All you need is love.

Realistic
3. I really love the togetherness in baseball.
That's a real true love.
8. Where there is love there is life.
9. Love conquers all things, except poverty and
toothache.
11. True love comes quietly, without banners or
flashing lights.
12. Love is pure and true, love knows no gender.
14. The course of true love never did run smooth.

26 Who asked me that?

Which day of the week do you prefer?	Who is the first person you fell in love with?
Where do you go to relax?	Do you think children spend too much time online?
Do you watch soap operas?	Can you remember the best teacher you've had?
Do you read a newspaper online every day?	Do you like watching documentaries?
What's your favourite building?	What are you doing next weekend?
Who is the most interesting person you know?	What objects do you always carry with you?
What do you want for your next birthday?	Which social media channels do you post on?
Do you listen to music when you travel by car?	What's your favourite colour?
What's the best book you've read?	What do you eat for breakfast?
Do you listen to podcasts in English?	Have you got any pets?
Have you got any brothers and sisters?	Which month of the year do you prefer?
What do you drink for breakfast?	What's the best film you've seen?
Do you eat your dinner in front of the TV?	Who is your favourite musician?
Do you listen to the radio in the morning?	Do you like talking on the phone?
What are you doing this evening?	What do you do to keep fit?
Do you read paperbacks or ebooks?	Have you got a good memory?
Do you like watching films on your phone?	Are you good at cooking?
What are your best qualities?	Do you like snow?

26 Who asked me that?

ACTIVITY
Groupwork: speaking, writing

AIM
To ask and answer the questions and then to remember who asked which questions

GRAMMAR AND FUNCTIONS
Reported speech: questions

Asked + clause

Direct questions and reported questions with question words (*who, what, how, which, where*) and without question words

VOCABULARY
General

TIME
30 minutes

PREPARATION
- Make one copy of the worksheet for each group of up to 12 students in the class. Cut the cards out as indicated.
- You will also need one blank sheet of paper for each group of three students.

PROCEDURE
1. If there are more than 12 students in the class, divide them into groups.

2. Give one card to each student in the class. These are the three questions they have to ask everybody in the class or group.

3. Now ask students to go round the class or group asking and answering questions. Tell them that they should listen to people's answers to the questions but that they do not have to remember them.

4. When they have done that, ask them to sit down in their groups and to work with two other members of the same group for the next part of the activity.

5. Ask each group of three to appoint a secretary to do the writing. The secretary should write the names of all the students in their group or class down the left-hand margin of a blank piece of paper.

6. Now tell students that they have ten minutes to work together and remember which questions were asked by each student in the class or group. They should write them down using the target language. For example:
Ahmed asked what we were doing the following weekend.
Geovana asked how we kept fit.
Yoko asked if we had any pets.

7. Ask students to stop writing after ten minutes and check their answers. Give one point for each question correctly allocated to a name. The winners are the students with the highest number of points.

FOLLOW-UP
1. Ask the class to think about the answers to their questions and report any that were interesting, funny or unusual.

27 Reported speech dominoes

15b	1a	1b	2a	2b	3a
She refused to …	'I think it's a really good idea for you to have a holiday.'	She encouraged him to …	'Yes, I agree – it's a brilliant film.'	She agreed that …	'I've made my decision – I'm not going out tonight.'

3b	4a	4b	5a	5b	6a
He decided not to …	'I will come home early this evening, I promise.'	She promised to …	'I'm sorry – I've forgotten your name.'	He apologised and said …	'Would you like to come to a music festival?'

6b	7a	7b	8a	8b	9a
He invited me to …	'Be careful. She's really annoyed.'	He warned me that …	'Shall I help you with your bags?'	She offered to …	'Don't forget to put it in your calendar.'

9b	10a	10b	11a	11b	12a
She reminded me to …	'I think you should go to the doctor.'	He advised me to …	'Could you please sit down and be quiet.'	She asked them to …	'I'm going to look for a new job.'

12b	13a	13b	14a	14b	15a
She told me that …	'Let's go to the cinema.'	He suggested that …	'Could you phone me tonight please?'	He asked me to …	'No, I don't want to see him.'

27 Reported speech dominoes

ACTIVITY
Pairwork: writing, speaking

AIM
To play a game of dominoes by matching direct and reported statements

GRAMMAR AND FUNCTIONS
Reported speech

Reporting verbs: *encourage, agree, decide, promise, apologise, invite, warn, offer, refuse, remind, advise, ask, tell, suggest*

VOCABULARY
General

TIME
35 to 45 minutes

PREPARATION
Make one copy of the worksheet and the 'How to play' sheet for each group of three students. Provide scissors.

PROCEDURE
1. Ask students to work in groups of three.

2. Give one copy of the worksheet to each group. Ask them to appoint a secretary to do the writing.

3. Explain that they are going to play a game of dominoes but that before they can start, they have to complete the sentences on the dominoes. Point out the way the dominoes are arranged and explain that they are numbered on the worksheet to show which sentences are connected.

4. Do the first sentence with the whole class. Ask students to look at domino 1a: *I think it's a really good idea for you to have a holiday.*
Ask them to complete the sentence in 1b by reporting the sentence in 1a: *She encouraged him to have a holiday.*

5. Now ask students to work in their groups to complete the b sentences. While they are doing this, go round and check that sentences are correct. Answer questions and offer help.

6. When they have finished, and you are satisfied that their sentences are correct (see ANSWERS), give each group a pair of scissors and ask them to cut the dominoes out as indicated. Make sure that students cut the numbers off the dominoes.

7. Each group should shuffle their dominoes and then give them to another group.

8. Before they start their game of dominoes, explain how to play using the instructions on the 'How to play' sheet. Students play the game. When they have finished one game, they can shuffle and play again.

27 Reported speech dominoes
How to play

1. Players take three dominoes each and leave the rest face down in a pile.

2. Player A plays any one of their dominoes face up.

3. The player on their left must then play one of their dominoes, making sure that one of the sentences on their domino matches one of the sentences on Player A's domino. For example:
(domino A) *I think it's a really good idea for you to have a holiday.*
(domino B) *She encouraged me to have a holiday.*

Players take it in turns to add dominoes in this way.

4. If a player cannot play one of their dominoes, they can take one from the top of the pile and put it down if they can. If the pile is finished, they miss a turn.

5. The first player to use all their dominoes wins.

27 Reported speech dominoes

ANSWERS

1b She encouraged him to have a holiday.

2b She agreed that it was a brilliant film.

3b He decided not to go out that night.

4b She promised to come home early that evening.

5b He apologised and said he was sorry he had forgotten their name.

6b He invited me to go to a music festival.

7b He warned me that she was really annoyed.

8b She offered to help me with my bags.

9b She reminded me to put it in my calendar.

10b He advised me to go to the doctor.

11b She asked them to sit down and be quiet.

12b She told me she was going to look for a new job.

13b He suggested that we go to the cinema.

14b He asked me to phone him that night.

15b She refused to see him.

28 Holiday crossword

Student A

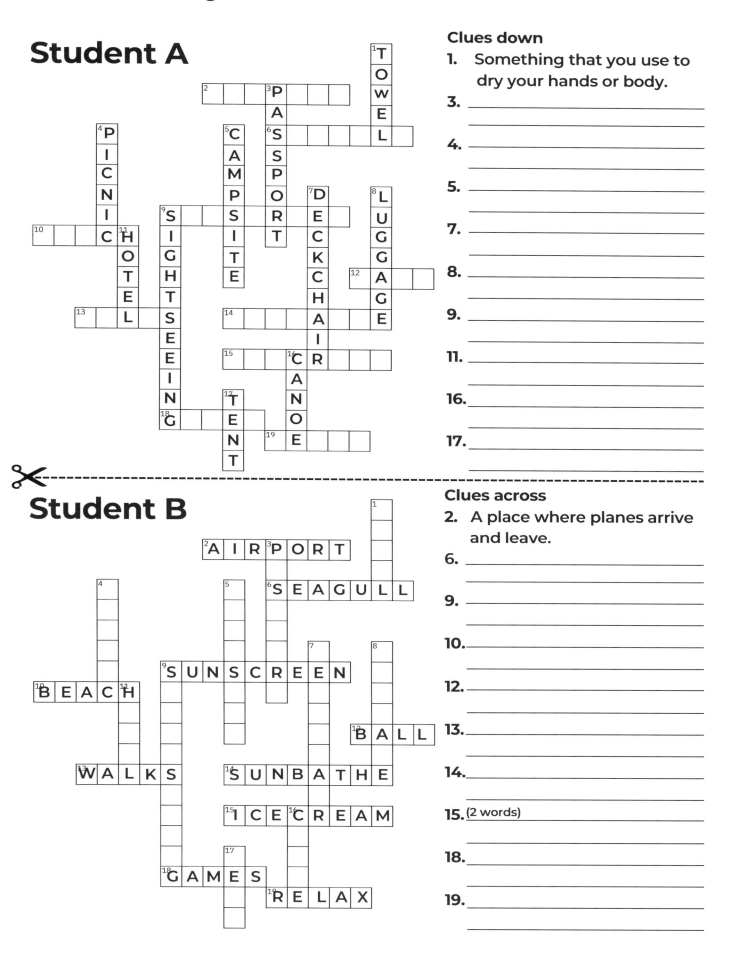

Clues down

1. Something that you use to dry your hands or body.
3. _____
4. _____
5. _____
7. _____
8. _____
9. _____
11. _____
16. _____
17. _____
   _____

Student B

Clues across

2. A place where planes arrive and leave.
6. _____
9. _____
10. _____
12. _____
13. _____
14. _____
15. (2 words) _____
   _____
18. _____
19. _____
   _____

28 Holiday crossword

ACTIVITY
Pairwork: speaking, writing

AIM
To write clues for a crossword and complete it

GRAMMAR AND FUNCTIONS
Defining relative clauses beginning with *who*, *that*, *which*, *where* or *whose*

VOCABULARY
Words associated with holidays

TIME
30 minutes

PREPARATION
Make one copy of the worksheet for each pair of students in the class and cut it in half as indicated.

PROCEDURE
1. Tell students that you are going to give them a definition of a word, and that they have to guess what the word is. Write *Something that you use to dry your hands and body* on the board. Elicit the answer *towel*. Tell students that they are going to write similar definitions of words as clues for a crossword. Tell them that the words are on the topic of holidays.

2. Divide the class into Group A and Group B.

3. Explain that you are going to give both groups the same crossword but that Group A will have the down words already written in and Group B will have the across words already written in. Their task is to write clues for the words written on their crosswords.

4. Give a copy of crossword A to each student in Group A and a copy of crossword B to each student in Group B.

5. Ask students to work with two or three students from the same group. They should invent and write clues for the words on their crossword in the spaces provided. All the students should write the clues on their own worksheet. Be on hand to help students with any words they don't know, and to make sure they write the definitions correctly.

6. When they have finished writing their clues, students should work with a partner from the other group (i.e. a student from Group A should work with a student from Group B). They must not show their crosswords to their partner.

7. Ask pairs to sit facing one another and take it in turns to ask each other for clues to the missing words on their own crossword. They should read out the clues they have written for their partner to guess the words and write in the missing words on their crosswords from the clues their partner gives them.

ANSWERS

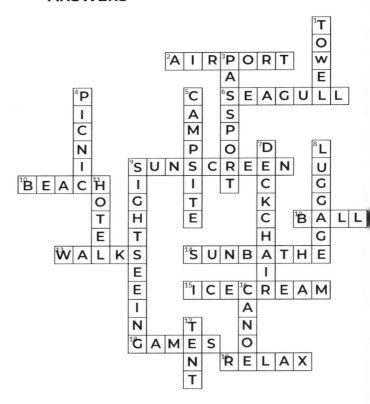

29 Jobs at home

The carpet is dirty.
(clean)

The walls are a horrible colour.
(decorate)

The grass is too long.
(cut)

The sink is blocked.
(unblock)

The computer has frozen.
(restart)

The plug is broken.
(replace)

The washing machine isn't working.
(fix)

The bin is full.
(empty)

The plant is dying.
(water)

The t-shirt is torn.
(repair)

The phone is dead.
(charge)

The windows are dirty.
(clean)

29 Jobs at home

ACTIVITY
Whole class: speaking
Mill drill. See the front of the book for detailed instructions and advice on using mill drills.

AIM
To speak to as many partners as possible about jobs that need doing around the home

GRAMMAR AND FUNCTIONS
Need + -ing and passive infinitive
Causative construction with *have* and *get*: *have something done*, *get something done*

VOCABULARY
Household jobs

TIME
15 to 20 minutes

PREPARATION
Make one copy of the worksheet for each group of up to 12 students. Cut the worksheet up into cards as indicated so that students have one card each. You will need to keep one card for yourself to demonstrate the activity.

PROCEDURE
1. If there are more than 12 students in the class, divide them into groups. Give one card to each student in the class. Keep one for yourself.

2. Check that each student understands the job that needs doing on their card. See Answers below.

3. Tell students that they are going to talk about jobs that need doing, using the word prompts on their card. Write an example dialogue on the board, indicating the kind of language the students should use. For example:
Student A: *The carpet needs cleaning.*
Student B: *Are you going to clean it yourself?*
Student A: *No, I'm going to have it cleaned.*

4. Demonstrate the activity with individual students using the card you kept for yourself. Tell students to hold their cards so the word prompts are facing them. Ask several pairs of students to demonstrate the activity to the whole class, using their cards as prompts.

5. Now ask students to go round the class and talk about the job that needs doing with as many different partners as possible, using their cards as prompts. In this part of the activity, students talk about the same job that needs doing each time they change partners.

6. When students have finished, ask them to exchange cards and to go round the class again, this time holding their cards the other way round so the word prompts are facing their partner. The students take it in turns to talk about jobs that need doing using the prompts on their partner's cards. In this part of the activity, students talk about a different job that needs doing each time they change partner.

7. Students continue in this way until they have spoken to as many different partners as possible.

FOLLOW-UP
Ask students to work in pairs and to talk about jobs that need doing in their own homes.

ANSWERS
The carpet needs cleaning.
The walls need decorating.
The grass needs cutting.
The sink needs unblocking.
The computer needs restarting.
The plug needs replacing.
The washing machine needs fixing.
The bin needs emptying.
The plant needs watering.
The t-shirt needs repairing.
The phone needs charging.
The windows need cleaning.

30 If I could change the world ...

(A) If I were my parents, ...

I'd make my children _____

_____

I'd let them _____

I wouldn't let them _____

_____

(B) If I were a teacher, ...

I'd make my pupils _____

_____

_____

I'd let them _____

I wouldn't let them _____

(C) If I were the manager of my country's football team, ...

I'd make my players _____

_____

_____

I'd let them _____

I wouldn't let them _____

(D) If I were the CEO of a big company, ...

I'd make my employees _____

_____

_____

I'd let them _____

I wouldn't let them _____

_____

30 If I could change the world ...

ACTIVITY
Whole class: writing, speaking

AIM
To write about and discuss what you would do if you were in different positions of authority

GRAMMAR AND FUNCTIONS
Make + noun/pronoun + infinitive to express obligation
Let + noun + infinitive to express permission
Not let to express prohibition

VOCABULARY
General

TIME
30 minutes

PREPARATION
Make one copy of the worksheet for each student in the class and cut it into sections A, B, C and D as indicated.

PROCEDURE
1. Explain to students that they are going to invent a list of rules they would impose if they were in positions of authority.

2. Give section A to each student in the class and ask them to think about what they would do if they were their own parents. They should then complete the sentences. For example:
If I were my parents, I'd make my children leave home when they were 18 / continue their studies for as long as possible / learn several languages / respect the environment.
I'd let them choose their own clothes / cook their own meals / bring their friends home.
I wouldn't let them spend hours on their phones / have a pet snake / come into the house with dirty boots on.

Make it clear to students that this is a light-hearted activity and encourage them to use their imagination.

3. Now ask students to compare their sentences with other students in the class.

4. Repeat the activity using sections B, C and D.

© **ELT Teacher 2 Writer. Written by Sue Kay.**

31 Spot the wrong word

1. A You look tired. What time did you come home last night?
   B Very late! I hope I didn't wake you up when I came in.

STUDENT A

2. Can you borrow me your tennis racket – I've forgotten mine.

3. A My brother needs cheering up so I'm going to bring him to the cinema tonight.
   B Oh, that's a good idea. Have a good time!

4. I thought it was okay to lend him my bicycle because he's usually very sensitive, but he forgot to lock it up and somebody stole it.

5. Doctors control the athletes before a race to make sure they haven't taken drugs.

6. I think I left my gloves on the bus.

7. I love sitting in a café seeing people walk past.

8. Please listen to the instructions carefully.

9. I've offered to do the shopping for my sister because she's expecting a baby and can't lift anything heavy.

10. I think it's going to rain. You can borrow my umbrella but try not to loose it this time.

---

1. A You look tired. What time did you go home last night?
   B Very late! I hope I didn't wake you up when I came in.

STUDENT B

2. Can you lend me your tennis racket – I've forgotten mine.

3. A My brother needs cheering up so I'm going to take him to the cinema tonight.
   B Oh, that's a good idea. Have a good time!

4. I thought it was okay to lend him my bicycle because he's usually very sensible, but he forgot to lock it up and somebody stole it.

5. Doctors check the athletes before a race to make sure they haven't taken drugs.

6. I think I forgot my gloves on the bus.

7. I love sitting in a café watching people walk past.

8. Please hear the instructions carefully.

9. I've offered to do the shopping for my sister because she's waiting for a baby and can't lift anything heavy.

10. I think it's going to rain. You can borrow my umbrella but try not to lose it this time.

31 Spot the wrong word

ACTIVITY
Pairwork: speaking

AIM
To identify and correct lexical mistakes in sentences

GRAMMAR AND FUNCTIONS
Revision

VOCABULARY
Words which are often confused

come – go, lend – borrow, bring – take, sensible – sensitive, check – control, leave – forget, watch – see, hear – listen to, expect – wait for, loose – lose

TIME
20 to 30 minutes

PREPARATION
Make one copy of the worksheet for each pair of students in the class and cut it in half as indicated.

PROCEDURE
1. Divide the class into equal numbers of Student As and Student Bs.

2. Give one copy of the Student A sentences to each Student A and one copy of the Student B sentences to each Student B.

3. Ask students to work in pairs of As and pairs of Bs. Tell them that some of their sentences are correct while some of them have an incorrect word in them. They should identify the incorrect words and correct them. The students should discuss the sentences in their pairs but all the students should write corrections on their own worksheets.

4. When they have finished, ask students to form pairs of Student A and Student B and compare their sentences. Student A has the correct word in sentences where Student B has the incorrect word and vice versa. This means that students should be able to correct one another at this stage.

© **ELT Teacher 2 Writer. Written by Sue Kay.**

5. Check that students have identified the incorrect words.

ANSWERS
1. What time did you <u>come</u> home last night? (The speaker is speaking from home.)
2. Can you <u>lend</u> me your tennis racket.
3. I'm going to <u>take</u> him to the cinema tonight. (The speaker is not at the cinema now.)
4. I thought it was okay to lend him my bicycle because he's usually very <u>sensible</u>.
5. Doctors <u>check</u> the athletes before a race to make sure they haven't taken drugs.
6. I think I <u>left</u> my gloves on the bus.
7. I love sitting in a café <u>watching</u> people walk past. (You *watch* things that change and move. *Seeing* is not always deliberate.)
8. Please <u>listen to</u> the instructions carefully. (*Listen to* suggests that you are paying attention. *Hearing* is not deliberate.)
9. She's <u>expecting</u> a baby and can't lift anything heavy.
10. You can borrow my umbrella but try not to <u>lose</u> it this time.

32 Describe it: game board

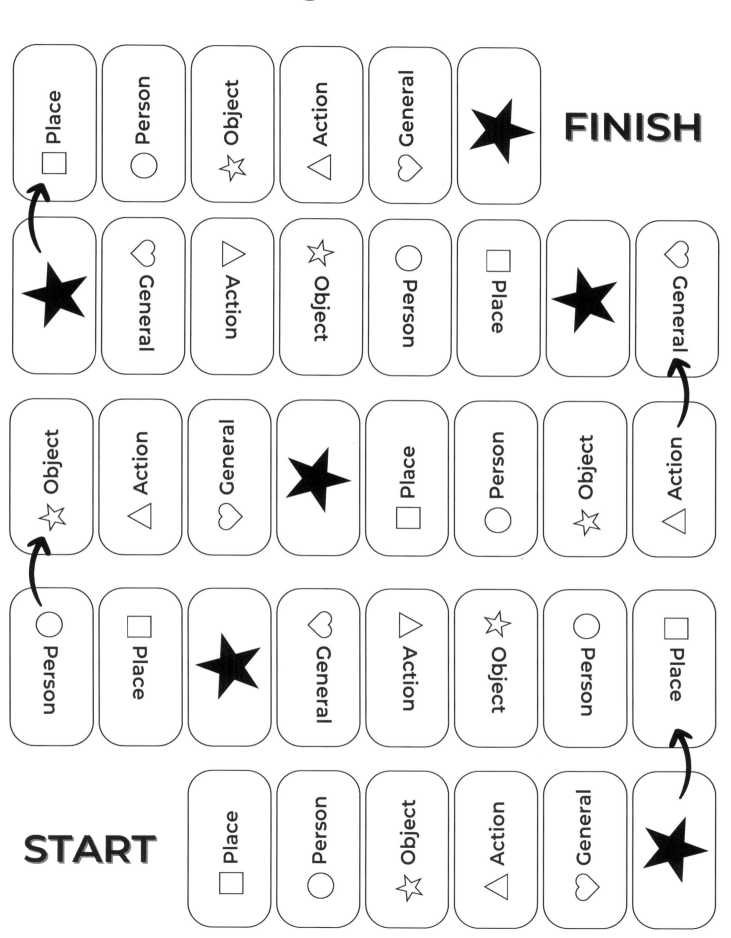

32 Describe it

ACTIVITY
Groupwork: speaking

AIM
To play a board game by describing and guessing
words

GRAMMAR AND FUNCTIONS
Describing things when you don't know the word:
It's a place where ..., someone who ..., something
that ..., something you use to ..., something you
do ...

VOCABULARY
Useful objects, general revision

TIME
30 to 40 minutes

PREPARATION
- Make one copy of the game board worksheet
  and one copy of the 'how to play' instructions
  for every six to eight students in the class.
- Make one copy of the cards worksheet for
  every six to eight students in the class and cut
  it out as indicated.
- Provide two counters for each group (one per
  team). Each group will also need a coin and
  access to a timer for timing the activity.

PROCEDURE
1. Ask students to work in groups of six to eight
and to divide each group into two teams.

2. Give one game board, one set of cards and
counters to each group. Make sure each group has
access to a timer.

3. Before students start playing the game, explain
how to play using the 'how to play' instructions
on the back of the cards page.

4. Students are ready to play the game. While they
are playing, go round to each group and check
they are playing correctly.

32 Describe it: cards

□ ★ hospital	□ hotel	□ bank
○ mechanic	○ tourist	○ neighbour
☆ radio	☆ ★ wheel	☆ door
△ sunbathe	△ laugh	△ travel
♡ easy	♡ wedding	♡ ★ anger
□ railway station	□ ★ restaurant	□ beach
○ referee	○ athlete	○ ★ builder
☆ ★ mobile phone	☆ mirror	☆ map
△ vote	△ sing	△ bake
♡ honest	♡ pizza	♡ patience
□ factory	□ forest	□ airport
○ electrician	○ politician	○ ★ author
☆ knife	☆ computer	☆ kettle
△ ★ drop	△ forgive	△ invent
♡ success	♡ ★ money	♡ funny
□ supermarket	□ nightclub	□ office
○ web designer	○ customer	○ lawyer
☆ ★ saucepan	☆ cap	☆ ★ passport
△ drive	△ hug	△ complain
♡ rap	♡ ★ horror film	♡ onion
□ school	□ museum	□ ★ cemetery
○ ★ actor	○ sister	○ gardener
☆ armchair	☆ ★ glasses	☆ vase
△ wait	△ recycle	△ borrow
♡ imaginative	♡ ambition	♡ hopeful
□ playground	□ ★ swimming pool	□ bathroom
○ ★ police officer	○ father	○ baby
☆ purse	☆ seat belt	☆ wallet
△ disappear	△ sail	△ ★ decorate
♡ impossible	♡ avocado	♡ special effects
□ mountains	□ market	□ art gallery
○ teacher	○ vet	○ hairdresser
☆ belt	☆ watch	☆ ★ paperback
△ ★ hug	△ learn	△ forget
♡ shampoo	♡ ★ embarrassed	♡ mug
□ library	□ island	□ garden
○ ★ friend	○ student	○ photographer
☆ carpet	☆ torch	☆ credit card
△ walk	△ ask	△ ★ drink
♡ tissue	♡ ★ cotton	♡ cabbage
□ home	□ castle	□ gym
○ carpenter	○ farmer	○ ★ TV presenter
☆ ★ backpack	☆ laptop	☆ bicycle
△ apologise	△ install	△ swim
♡ summer	♡ ★ remote control	♡ strawberry

32 Describe it

HOW TO PLAY

1. Put the game board in the middle of the table and place the cards in a pile face down.

2. Each team puts their counter on the Place box next to the START and teams toss a coin to see who starts the game.

3. Player 1 picks up a card from the top of the pile and finds the word corresponding to the Place category.

4. Player 1 now has one minute to describe the word to the rest of the team. A player from the other team should time one minute exactly.

5. When the rest of the team have guessed a word correctly, Player 1 can take another card and describe another word in the same category. They can repeat the process as many times as possible within the minute time limit.

6. After one minute, Player 1 stops and moves their team's counter along the board according to the number of words the team guessed correctly. The box they land on determines the category of words they will describe when they have their next turn.

7. If a player lands on a square with a ★ on it, the player has to pick cards and describe the words with a ★ next to them. Members of both teams are allowed to guess the words, and move their team's counter according to the number of words they have guessed correctly.

8. Players put the cards at the bottom of the pile when they have finished with them.

9. Teams take it in turns to play and players take it in turns to be describers and guessers.

10. The first team to reach FINISH is the winner.

33 How many uses can you think of?

You can use an old toothbrush …

_____
_____
_____
_____

You can use a teaspoon …

_____
_____
_____
_____

You can use an old newspaper …

_____
_____
_____
_____

You can use a coat hanger …

_____
_____
_____
_____

You can use an empty bottle …

_____
_____
_____
_____

You can use a hair dryer …

_____
_____
_____
_____

You can use a lipstick …

_____
_____
_____
_____

You can use a saucepan …

_____
_____
_____
_____

You can use a paperclip …

_____
_____
_____
_____

You can use a tennis racket …

_____
_____
_____
_____

33 How many uses can you think of

ACTIVITY
Groupwork: writing, speaking

AIM
To invent unusual uses for ordinary objects

GRAMMAR AND FUNCTIONS
Infinitive of purpose: *to* + infinitive to say how you do something

By + *-ing* to say how you do something

Use it as a ...

Giving advice: *If* + present simple to describe a problem and what to do about it

VOCABULARY
Everyday objects and activities

TIME
20 to 30 minutes

PREPARATION
Make one copy of the worksheet for each group of three to five students.

PROCEDURE
1. Ask students to work in groups of three to five.

2. Tell them that they are going to invent unusual uses for everyday objects, for example, a piece of chewing gum. Elicit some suggestions from the class, encouraging them to use their imagination. Ask them to clarify where necessary, for example:
You can use a piece of chewing gum ...

... to make friends. If you give someone half a piece of chewing gum, they'll think you're really nice.

... to stick things together (by chewing the gum to make it sticky).

... to unblock your ears when you're taking off in an aeroplane (by chewing it).

... to freshen your breath when it isn't convenient to clean your teeth, etc.

3. Give one copy of the worksheet to each group of students and ask them to appoint a secretary to do the writing.

4. Tell students that they've got ten minutes to think of as many uses as possible for the objects on their worksheet and to write them down in the spaces provided. The group that thinks of the highest number of unusual uses will be the winners. Encourage them to be as imaginative or as amusing as they like.

5. While they are doing this, go round the class and help students with any language problems they may have. If they're having difficulty inventing new uses for the objects, you may like to give them some suggestions. See below.

6. Stop the activity after ten minutes. Ask groups to take turns to read out their uses for an old toothbrush. They score one point for each unusual use, provided they can explain it to the satisfaction of the other students if necessary.

7. Repeat the process for each object on the worksheet. The group with the highest score at the end of the activity are the winners.

POSSIBLE ANSWERS
Old toothbrush: clean the sink, polish your shoes, create a painting

Teaspoon: make music by using it as a drumstick, make jewellery, make a shoehorn

Old newspaper: clean windows, wrap a parcel, start a fire

Coat hanger: unblock a sink, support a plant, hang up a towel

Empty bottle: use as a vase for flowers, use it to collect ideas in, use it as a candle holder

Hair dryer: defrost food, dust bookshelves, clean a keyboard

Lipstick: write a sign for a demo, give to children for art, use to paint blood on your face

Saucepan: store pens and pencils, plant a houseplant, make music (or a loud noise) by using it as a drum

Paperclip: release a SIM card from a phone, mark a page in a book, hold a bunch of flowers together

Tennis racket: use it as a photo frame, hang earrings on it, use it as a tray

34 If you come here: information

Student A

Volunteering on an organic farm in Tuscany, Italy

Tuscany is popular with tourists, and it's easy to see why. The hilly countryside is wonderful with its hilltop towns, ancient castles and rows of cypress trees. In the green valleys, there are fields of wheat, olive trees and vineyards. The climate is Mediterranean, with mild wet winters and hot dry summers. If you volunteer here, you'll find the Italian farming families friendly and welcoming. Your day will begin at 8am and you'll work in the fields until 12.30. This work can be hard and physical, but you'll also learn a lot about plants and organic farming methods. Then you'll have the rest of the day off to explore the countryside, swim in the hot springs or visit the historic cities of Florence, Pisa or Siena. You'll live in a house with other volunteers from all over the world, and you'll cook and eat all your meals together. The food is typically Italian with a lot of pasta and fresh vegetables. And if you're a fan of nature, you'll find Tuscany is a great place to go birdwatching – there are almost 300 different kinds of birds to see.

Student B

Volunteering on a small family farm in Patagonia, Argentina

If you want to get away from the crowds, you'll love Patagonia! It covers the southern part of Argentina and has one of the lowest populations anywhere in the world. The environment is wild: a mixture of forests, glaciers, mountains, rivers and volcanoes. The weather can be very windy, but this remote region is a true paradise for adventurous backpackers and nature-lovers. If you volunteer on a small farm in in Patagonia, you will be part of a small group of two or three visitors, and you'll live in a simple family home as part of the family. It's an ideal opportunity to improve your Spanish. You'll wake up at sunrise and work six hours a day, six days a week with the family. Jobs will include gardening, picking cherries and taking care of horses. You'll eat all your meals with the family and if you love meat, you'll be happy. Your diet will consist of a lot of meat, especially lamb, and vegetables from the garden. If you want to explore the region, you'll do it on horseback. There are no dangerous snakes or spiders in Patagonia, but you may be lucky enough to see a puma, the rare mountain lion.

Student C

Volunteering on a yoga retreat in Sydney, Australia

When you think of Sydney, you probably think of beaches, shopping and entertainment. But volunteering at the Yoga Wellness Centre offers you the chance to experience a different side of the busy city. The Centre is situated 30 minutes from the sea in beautiful gardens on the outskirts of Sydney. People from all over the world come here for peace and quiet and the chance to reconnect with their body. If you volunteer at the Yoga Wellness Centre, you'll work in the garden and the kitchen. Summers are hot and humid, so you'll start work at 6.15am and then have a one-hour break for breakfast at 8am. After that you'll work until lunchtime. You'll follow a vegetarian diet. In the afternoon, you can join yoga classes or you can enjoy a swim in the nearby river, or drive to the beach. If you want to see some typical Australian animals, you'll be able to visit one of the many national parks around Sydney where you may spot koalas, kangaroos and wallabies. Accommodation is in a camping area, and if you stay here, you will need to use your own tent.

34 If you come here

ACTIVITY
Groupwork: reading, writing, speaking

AIM
To read information and to write notes about it
To choose a place you want to visit

GRAMMAR AND FUNCTIONS
First conditional to talk about a likely situation
and to talk about its result

VOCABULARY
Description of places, scenery and lifestyle

TIME
40 to 50 minutes

PREPARATION
Make one copy of the Information worksheet for
every three students in the class and cut it into
sections A, B and C as indicated. Make one copy
of the Chart worksheet for each student in the
class.

PROCEDURE
1. Ask students to work in groups of three.
Explain that they have decided to do voluntary
work through a company that organises
volunteers around the world. They are going to
decide where their group will go to do this
voluntary work and they have three places to
choose from.

2. Write the names of the three places on the
board and ask students to spend a few moments
brainstorming what sort of experiences they think
they will have if they go to each of the places.
Tuscany, Italy / Patagonia, Argentina / Sydney,
Australia

3. Give sections A, B and C from the Information
worksheet to each group and ask each student to
read one section without showing it to the other
members of their group. Explain that each
member of the group has got information about
one of the places.

4. Give a copy of the Chart worksheet to each
student in the class and ask them to write notes
about their place in the spaces provided.

5. When they have finished writing notes, tell
them that each student in the group is now
responsible for describing their place while the
rest of the group takes notes in the relevant
spaces on their chart.

6. When they have done that, they should discuss
the three places and come to a group decision
about which of the places they are going to visit.

7. Tell students to work with others from
different groups and tell them about the decision
their group has made.

OPTION
Throughout the activity students can work in
pairs rather than individually. That is, in each
group there are two Student As, two Student Bs,
etc.

34 If you come here: chart

	Tuscany	Patagonia	Sydney
Landscape / weather			
Wildlife			
Daily routine / jobs			
Accommodation / food			
Places to visit / things to do			

34 If you come here: answers

	Tuscany	Patagonia	Sydney
Landscape / weather	Hilly, hilltop towns, ancient castles and rows of cypress trees. Green valleys, fields of wheat, olive trees and vineyards. Mediterranean climate; mild wet winters and hot dry summers.	Wild: forests, glaciers, mountains, rivers and volcanoes. The weather can be very windy.	Beautiful gardens on the outskirts of Sydney. Near the sea. Hot humid summers.
Wildlife	Almost 300 species of birds	There are no dangerous snakes or spiders in Patagonia, but you may be lucky enough to see a puma, the rare mountain lion.	You may spot koalas, kangaroos and wallabies in one of the national parks.
Daily routine / jobs	8am until 12.30 you'll work in the fields. Rest of the day off. The work can be hard and physical, but you'll also learn a lot about plants and organic farming methods.	You'll wake up at sunrise and work six hours a day, six days a week with the family. Jobs will include gardening, picking cherries and taking care of horses.	You'll work in the garden and the kitchen. You'll start work at 6.15am and then have a one-hour break for breakfast at 8am. After that you'll work until lunchtime.
Accommodation / food	You'll live in a house with other volunteers from all over the world. Cook and eat together. Typical Italian food: pasta and fresh vegetables.	You'll live in a simple family home as part of a small group and the family. Your diet will consist of a lot of meat, especially lamb, and vegetables from the garden.	You'll follow a vegetarian diet. Accommodation is in a camping area, and you will need to use your own tent.
Places to visit / things to do	Explore the countryside, swim in hot springs or visit the historic cities of Florence, Pisa or Siena.	Improve your Spanish. Explore on horseback.	In the afternoon, you can join yoga classes or you can enjoy a swim in the nearby river, or drive to the beach. If you want to see some Australian wildlife, you can visit one of the many national parks.

35 A mysterious connection

Student A

Sam dreamt nearly every night and the same person appeared in all his dreams. He had never met the man he dreamt about, but in his dreams, he felt as if he knew him well.

_____
_____
_____

Sailors from all over the world had been taking part in the Transatlantic yacht race and now it was nearly over. But that night, there had been a violent storm and one of the boats and its sailor had disappeared.

_____
_____

He hurried out to buy the morning newspapers. Pictures of the missing sailor, Simon Shepherd, were all over the front pages. He recognised the face of the man he had dreamt about so often.

_____
_____
_____

He had recovered from his accident when they met some time later. They looked at one another and both had the strangest feeling that they were looking into a mirror.

_____
_____

They had both been born in London on exactly the same date. On that date, a young woman had died after giving birth to identical twins.

_____
_____
_____

Student B

_____
_____
_____

When he woke up that morning, he knew something had happened. When he switched on the radio he was not surprised to hear the news.

_____
_____
_____

In his dream he had seen the man in the stormy seas and now he was sure that this was the man who had disappeared at sea. He also knew that he had survived.

_____
_____
_____

A few days later, he heard that Simon had been found and was now back in England in hospital. He had to meet him.

_____
_____
_____

Since the accident, Sam had been making some enquiries and had managed to trace the incredible link between himself and Simon Shepherd, the man from his dreams.

_____
_____
_____

As the woman had no other family, her babies had been adopted. At the time, nobody had wanted to adopt twins and so Sam and his twin brother had been separated at birth and adopted by different parents.

35 A mysterious connection

ACTIVITY
Pairwork: speaking, writing
Mutual dictation

AIM
To dictate part of a story and to write down what your partner dictates to you

GRAMMAR AND FUNCTIONS
Past perfect simple to talk about one action in the past which happened before another action in the past
Past perfect continuous when you want to focus on an action which was in progress up to or near a time in the past, rather than a completed event

VOCABULARY
Narrative

TIME
20–30 minutes

PREPARATION
Make one copy of the worksheet for each pair of students in the class. Cut out sections A and B as indicated.

PROCEDURE
1. Tell students that they are going to read a story about a man called Sam. Tell them that you are going to give them a text with some missing information.

2. Ask students to work in pairs of Student A and Student B.

3. Give one copy of text A to each Student A and one copy of text B to each Student B. Tell them not to show their part of the story to their partner. Explain that their partner has the part of the story which is missing from their own version.

4. Ask students to take it in turns to dictate lines of the story and to write them down in the spaces provided on their worksheet.

5. When they have finished, ask students to compare completed texts, which should be identical.

FOLLOW-UP
Ask students if they know any similar stories, either true ones or from fiction.

36 Holiday choices

a very different culture   loud discos   local food   holiday romance

self-catering   long walks   crowds   siestas   water sports

fast food   unspoilt nature   sunbathing   all-inclusive

no wifi   local culture   green fields   hot sun   guided tours

alone   peace and quiet   no timetable   with friends   cool weather

mountain sports   big, modern hotels   with your family

non-stop entertainment   camping   travelling by public transport

lots of tourists from your own country   in the middle of nowhere   organised tours to places of historical interest

The holiday of my dreams	The holiday of my nightmares

36 Holiday choices

ACTIVITY
Pairwork: speaking

AIM
To categorise vocabulary and to discuss what you look for in a holiday

GRAMMAR AND FUNCTIONS
My holiday priorities are …
I'm not a fan of …
When I'm on holiday I like/don't like to …
If x happened, I'd …

VOCABULARY
Holidays

TIME
20 to 30 minutes

PREPARATION
Make one copy of the worksheet for each student in the class.

PROCEDURE
1. Write the column headings from the worksheet where students can see them, and brainstorm what aspects of a holiday turn it into a dream holiday or a nightmare holiday for students.

2. Give one copy of the worksheet to each student in the class and ask then to put some of the words and expressions on the worksheet under the headings according to their personal opinion. They do not have to use all the words and expressions, only those which they personally associate with a good or a bad holiday.

3. Ask students to add anything else they can think of under the headings.

4. Ask them to compare their worksheets with one or more partners and note any similarities or differences.

5. Ask students to tell each other about the best or worst holiday they've ever had.

37 Dear Sue

Dear Sue
I've been offered a job that I really want but it means moving from the place where I grew up.

Should I take the job and move, or should I stay where my family and friends are?

Dear Sue
My flatmate is really hard to live with.

What can I do?

Dear Sue
We've got really noisy neighbours.

What can we do about it?

Dear Sue
I'm getting married next month and everything's arranged but I can't forget what happened at my sister's wedding two years ago.

How can I make sure the same thing doesn't happen again?

Dear Sue
I've fallen out with my parents because of a stupid argument.

Can you give me some advice?

Dear Sue
While I was on holiday last month I got involved with someone.

Should I stay in touch or should I break it off now?

37 Dear Sue

ACTIVITY
Pairwork: speaking, writing

AIM
To practise talking about relationships

GRAMMAR AND FUNCTIONS
Expressions for giving advice:
If I were you I'd …
I think you should/ought to …
In my opinion, you should/ought to …

VOCABULARY
Personal relationships and life in general

TIME
30 to 40 minutes

PREPARATION
Make one copy of the worksheet for each group of 12 students and cut it into sections as indicated.

PROCEDURE
1. Ask students to suggest where people can get advice if they have a problem. Explain what an agony aunt is (a person who gives advice to people when they write to an advice column in a magazine, on social media, or in a podcast, because they have a problem they want help with).

2. If there are more than 12 students in the class, divide them into groups and ask them to work with a partner from the same group. Give each pair of students in the group a problem section.

3. Explain that each pair of students in the group has a different beginning and ending of a problem sent to an agony aunt and that they are going to invent the missing details and write them in the space provided. Encourage students to be as imaginative or as amusing as they like and be on hand to offer help as this is quite a challenging task.

4. When they have finished, ask pairs to give their problem to the pair of students on their left.

5. Ask students to read the problem they have received and to write a reply, giving advice. Encourage them to use the target language at this stage of the activity.

6. When they have done that, ask students to keep their replies and give the original problem to the pair of students on their left. Pairs write a reply to the problem they have just received.

7. Repeat the activity until pairs have written replies to several problems.

8. Now ask pairs to give their replies back to the students who wrote the original problems. Students read the replies and choose the best advice.

38 What went wrong?

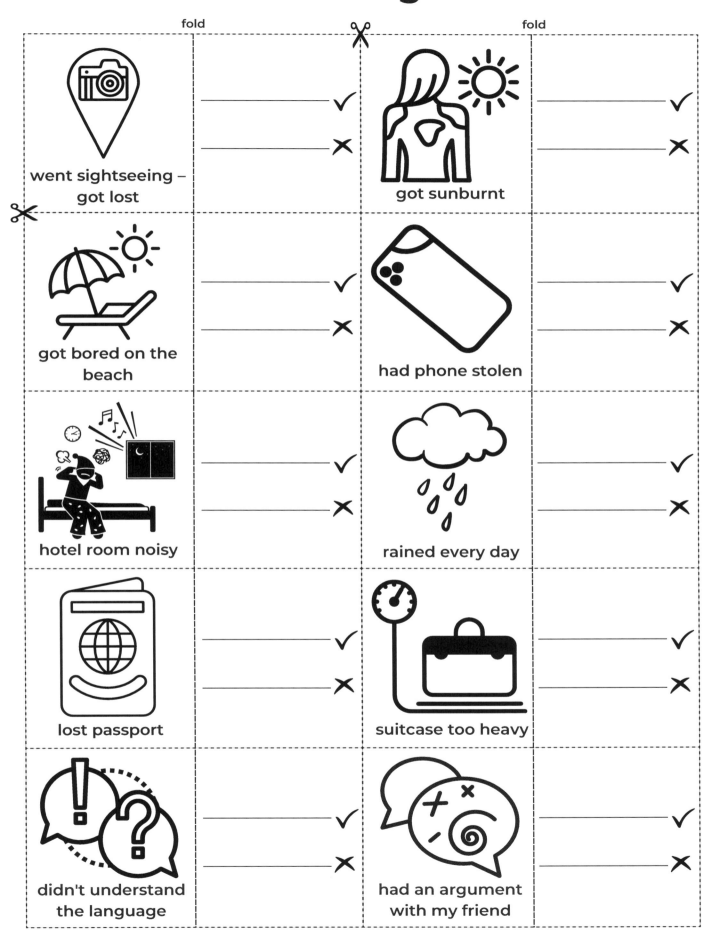

went sightseeing –
got lost

got sunburnt

got bored on the
beach

had phone stolen

hotel room noisy

rained every day

lost passport

suitcase too heavy

didn't understand
the language

had an argument
with my friend

38 What went wrong?

ACTIVITY
Whole class: speaking
Mill drill. See the front of the book for detailed instructions and advice on using mill drills.

AIM
To speak to as many partners as possible; commenting on things which went wrong on holiday

GRAMMAR AND FUNCTIONS
Past modals: *should have* and *shouldn't have*

VOCABULARY
Holiday activities, travel

TIME
20 to 30 minutes

PREPARATION
Make one copy of the worksheet for each group of up to ten students. Cut the worksheet up into cards as indicated so that students have one card each. You will need to keep one card for yourself to demonstrate the activity.

PROCEDURE
1. If there are more than ten students in the class, divide them into groups. Give one card to each student in the class. Keep one for yourself.

2. Make sure each student understands that the prompt on their card describes something that went wrong on holiday.

3. Ask students to think about what the person should and shouldn't have done. They should write one thing the person should have done next to the tick and one thing they shouldn't have done next to the cross. For example:
(went sightseeing – got lost)
You should have used Maps on your phone. ✓
You shouldn't have gone on your own. ✗

4. When they have done that, ask students to fold their card so that the picture is on one side and their comments are on the other side.

5. Tell students that they are going to talk about what went wrong using the words and pictures on their cards as prompts. Write an example dialogue so students can see it, indicating the language they should use. For example:
Student A: *What went wrong?*
Student B: (looking at the picture and words on their own card) *I went sightseeing and got lost.*
Student A: (looking at what's written on the back of Student B's card) *Oh dear, you should have looked at Maps on your phone and you shouldn't have gone on your own.*

6. Demonstrate the activity with individual students. Tell students to hold their cards so the picture is facing them and the side they have written on is facing their partner. Ask several pairs of students to demonstrate the activity to the whole class, using their cards as prompts.

7. Now ask students to go round the class or group and talk to as many different partners as possible, using their cards as prompts. In this stage of the activity, students describe the same thing that went wrong several times.

8. When students have finished, ask them to exchange cards and to go round the class again, this time holding their cards the other way round so the word and picture prompt is facing their partner. They take it in turns to describe what went wrong using the picture and word prompts on their partner's cards. In this stage of the activity, the students describe a different thing that went wrong each time they change partner.

OPTION
For further practice, the cards can be used for the following activity.
Ask students to go round the class holding their cards so that they are concealed from the partners. They should read out their comment in the third person and their partner should guess what went wrong. For example:
Student A: *He should have looked at Maps on his phone and he shouldn't have gone on his own.*
Student B: *Did he get lost?*

© **ELT Teacher 2 Writer. Written by Sue Kay.**

39 If only I'd taken more chances

Elaine Maggs, 87, looks back on her life ...

 I've always been a sensible person, one of those people who never goes anywhere without a thermometer, a hot water bottle, a raincoat and a parachute.

Now I wish I'd made more mistakes.
I wish I'd relaxed more and been sillier.
I wish I hadn't taken everything so seriously.
I wish I'd taken more trips, climbed more mountains, swum more rivers, watched more sunsets, eaten more ice cream and picked more daisies.

If only I'd taken more chances. 99

Now that you are 87 years old, what are your regrets?

I've always been a _____ sort of person.

I wish I had been more _____

_____

I wish I had been less _____

_____

I wish I had _____

_____

I wish I hadn't _____

_____

If only _____

_____

Now go out and do all those things so that you won't have any regrets when you're 87!

39 If only I'd taken more chances

ACTIVITY
Whole class: reading, writing, speaking

AIM
To imagine you're 87 years old and to talk about past regrets

GRAMMAR AND FUNCTIONS
Expressing regrets about the past with *I wish / If only* + past perfect

VOCABULARY
General

TIME
30 minutes

PREPARATION
Make one copy of the worksheet for each student in the class.

PROCEDURE
1. Display the picture of Elaine Maggs and ask students to read what she says and make comments about it.

2. Give one copy of the worksheet to each student in the class and ask them to imagine that they are 87 years old.

3. Tell them that, now that they're 87, they should look back on their lives, think about their regrets, and complete the unfinished sentences on their worksheet.

4. When they have done that, ask them to compare their sentences with other students in the class if they wish.

5. Finally, tell students that they should go out and do all the things they might regret not doing when they're older.

OPTION
Ask students to complete the sentences on their worksheet from the point of view of somebody else: either somebody they know or a famous person.

40 Imagine

If I hadn't come here today, I would have _____

_____

_____

If I'd found €100 in the street today, I would have _____

_____

_____

If I hadn't come here today, I would have _____

_____

_____

If I'd met my hero, I would have

_____

_____

_____

If I'd had time this week, I would have_____

_____

_____

If I'd gone to a party last night, I would have_____

_____

_____

If I'd been born 20 years earlier, I would have _____

_____

_____

If I'd listened to my friends, I would have_____

_____

_____

If I'd followed my parents' advice, I would have _____

_____

_____

If I'd met my great-great grandparents, I would have_____

_____

_____

If I'd won the lottery recently, I would have_____

_____

_____

If I'd checked my messages, I would have _____

_____

_____

40 Imagine

ACTIVITY
Whole class: writing, speaking

AIM
To write sentences about imaginary situations in the past and their results
To pick sentences out of a hat and find out who wrote them by asking questions

GRAMMAR AND FUNCTIONS
Third conditional to talk about an imaginary or unlikely situation in the past and to describe its result

VOCABULARY
General

TIME
20 minutes

PREPARATION
Make one copy of the worksheet for each group of three to four students in the class and cut it up as indicated. You will need a hat or a box for this activity (or two containers if there are 20 or more students in the class).

PROCEDURE
1. Choose one of the unfinished sentences from the worksheet and write it on the board. Elicit possible ways of completing the sentence. For example: *If I hadn't come here today, I'd have gone to the gym.*

2. Ask students to work in groups of three or four for the first part of the activity. Give one set of unfinished sentences to each group and ask students to spread out the pieces of paper face-down and to take three each.

3. Ask them to complete their sentences in any way they like. They should not write their names or let their neighbours see what they are writing.

4. Students now all work together as a class. Put the hat (or box) in the middle of the room. If there are 20 or more students in the class, divide them into two groups and put a hat in the middle of each group. Ask students to fold up their completed sentences and put them in the hat.

5. Mix up the sentences in the hat and then tell students that they are all going to stand up, take a sentence each and find out who wrote it. Demonstrate by taking a piece of paper from the hat and reading the sentence out. For example: *If I hadn't come here today, I'd have gone to the gym.* Elicit the question they will need to ask to find out who wrote the sentence: *If you hadn't come here today, would you have gone to the gym?* Ask the question until you find the person who wrote the sentence. Even though students may answer *yes* to the question, they are looking for the person who wrote it, and may need to ask, *Did you write this sentence?*

6. Before students start the activity, point out that the second clause of most sentences begins with *I would have* or *I wouldn't have* and that, although it should be written without contraction, it is pronounced *I'd've / I wouldn't've*. Practise this.

7. Now ask students to stand up and take a piece of paper each from the hat. If they choose their own sentence, they should return it and pick again. Students are now ready to go round the class or group asking questions. All the students in the class do this simultaneously. Go round and offer help with formulating the questions correctly.

8. When a student finds the person who wrote the sentence, they should write the person's name on the piece of paper, keep it, and take another one from the hat. Students repeat the activity until there are no sentences left in the hat.

9. Ask students to sit down and count the number of completed sentences they have collected. The student with the most sentences is the winner.

10. Ask students to report back to the class on what they found out during the activity. For example: *If Monica hadn't come here today, she would have stayed in bed.*

Other books by ELT Teacher 2 Writer

Visit eltteacher2writer.co.uk for further information.

A Lexicon For ELT Professionals
How ELT Publishing Works
How To Adapt Authentic Texts ○
How To Plan A Book ○
How To Write And Deliver Talks
How To Write Audio And Video Scripts ◊
How To Write Business English Materials □
How To Write CLIL Materials
How To Write Corporate Training Materials □
How To Write Critical Thinking Activities ◊
How To Write EAP Materials □
How To Write ESOL Materials □
How To Write ESP Materials □
How To Write Exam Preparation Materials
How To Write Film And Video Activities
How To Write Graded Readers
How To Write Grammar Presentations And Practice ○
How To Write Inclusive Materials ○
How To Write Primary Materials
How To Write Pronunciation Activities ○
How To Write Reading And Listening Activities ◊
How To Write Secondary Materials
How To Write Speaking Activities ◊
How To Write Teacher's Books
How To Write Vocabulary Presentations And Practice ◊ ○
How To Write Worksheets
How To Write Writing Activities ◊

How To Write Excellent ELT Materials: The Skills Series
This book contains the six titles marked ◊ above.

How To Write Excellent ELT Materials: The ESP Series
This book contains the five titles marked □ above.

How to Write Excellent ELT Materials: The Basics Series
This book contains the six titles marked ○ above.

Reward Resource Pack Revival: Intermediate
By Sue Kay
© 2023 ELT Teacher 2 Writer
eltteacher2writer.co.uk

Sue and ELT Teacher 2 Writer would like:

- to pay tribute to Simon Greenall. Simon asked Sue to write the original *Reward Resource Packs* to accompany the Reward series published by Heinemann.
- to thank Catherine Smith for being a brilliant editor and helping to shape the original Resource Packs.
- to thank Macmillan Education and Jill Florent for assigning copyright of the *Reward Resource Packs* to us and enabling us to update and republish them.
- to thank all the teachers around the world who have given such positive feedback over the years. It is this love for the *Reward Resource Packs* that has given us the impetus to update and republish them.

Printed in Great Britain
by Amazon

43941396R00055